Get Accepted Into Architecture School

For more information on Architecture Schools, please visit our website at:
http://www.myschoolofarchitecture.com

Cover design: Arious Designs

Get Accepted Into Architecture School

Luke Glasscock

Foreword by: Marjorie K. Dickstein, AIA

www.myschoolofarchitecture.com

DEDICATION

To those who have supported me through every step of life's journey, I thank you.

To those who struggle to pursue goals others say are unattainable, I am inspired by you.

To my wife and children, who love me for my faults and ask nothing more of me than time, all of my successes can be attributed to you.

CONTENTS

FOREWORD

If you become an architect you'll probably meet a lot of people who will tell you that they once wanted to be architects too, but that they didn't think they could get into architecture school because they weren't good at math—or drawing (this was what intimidated me most)—or some other single skill that became their reason to give up their architectural aspirations before they pursued them very far. As it turns out, in my typical workday there's hardly ever any extraordinarily difficult math, and architecture school was a very good place to learn how to draw. While there's no shortage of valid reasons to decide not to become an architect, fear of the admissions process isn't a very good one, and I don't think anybody with a strong interest in architecture should give up before finding out more about what an architect really does and investigating what their own steps could be to become one.

Luke's book breaks the architecture school application process into step-by-step actionable items, based on his own successful experience. His checklist approach presents a manageable plan for moving forward, and he provides various alternative routes to serve different strengths, backgrounds, and entry points.

This book provides an overview of what some of your first steps could be toward your goal of attending architecture school. But first, before you select schools to which to apply and begin your application process, I have a few checklist items to add to the very beginning:

1. Learn about what architects do. Talk to as many architects as you can. See if you can arrange an internship or if you

can shadow an architect at his or her firm. Read publications geared toward practicing architects. Many people imagine that architects draw, build cardboard and/or digital models, and do math. But some don't realize that many architects also spend a considerable amount of time writing, researching, meeting, marketing, and managing. I enjoy most of aspects of the design process as much as building models and drawing. Some architects don't. Some architects work in small enough roles in large enough firms that most of the time they can do only the tasks that they most enjoy. Other architects work in small enough firms that they get to—or have to—do everything, all the time.

2. Learn what architecture students do. Visit architecture schools, both during times when students are working in their studios and during critiques of their work. Schools' open houses are great for getting an overview of the curriculum, seeing the spaces, meeting some faculty, and seeing students' work—but to get the most complete picture it can also be helpful to visit when they're not expecting you. Talk to current students—and not just the enthusiastic and articulate ones who greet you at the open house. Seek out the students who are frantically working toward impossible deadlines in the depths of their studios, and even the disgruntled ones who want to tell you about why they're thinking of dropping out. Ask the schools for names and contact information for alumni, and ask them about their experiences in the architecture school, finding employment, and working in field after graduation.

3. Learn what comes after architecture school on the path to becoming an architect. All US States license architects. In

most cases obtaining a license requires three phases—graduation from an accredited architecture degree program is the first. Architecture school is usually followed by an internship phase in one or more architecture firms that typically takes 3 or more years after graduation to complete. The last phase is a series of examination divisions (currently 7). Ask prospective schools whether they have statistics on how many of their grads stay in the field, how many eventually become licensed architects, and how long that typically takes. Visit the National Council of Architectural Registration Boards (www.ncarb.org) for more information about states' current licensing requirements.

In addition to confirming your interest in applying to architecture schools, addressing the above checklist items can also help you to identify your interests and aptitude for aspects of the profession, select schools that best match your goals, and demonstrate to those schools through your portfolio and your personal statement exactly how and why you belong there.

This book provides firsthand knowledge from the author's own application process and student life, formatted as a framework for you to adapt and fill in with your own work as you assemble your applications. Approached step by step, acceptance to architecture school is an attainable goal for an informed and confident applicant.

Marjorie K. Dickstein, AIA

*Master of Architecture, Yale University

PATHS TO ARCHITECTURE SCHOOL

Program Options

There are three degree options for studying architecture: pre-professional, professional, and post-professional.

A pre-professional degree is usually some form of a Bachelor of Art/Science degree that allows the individual to later continue on to receive a Professional degree after they have graduated. It is designed to prepare the architecture student for the professional degree, which is needed to receive your architecture license in most states. A pre-professional degree usually takes four years to complete.

A professional degree is one that is accredited by the National Architectural Accrediting Board (NAAB). The degrees in this area are: Bachelor of Architecture (B. Arch), Master of Architecture (M. Arch), and Doctor of Architecture (D. Arch). I will not go into much detail here, as I will be explaining it in full a little later on. I have only listed NAAB-accredited degrees in this book.

Post-professional degrees are graduate degrees offered to people who have already completed a professional degree. These are not always accredited by the NAAB. Because the person must have a professional degree, the post-professional degrees are offered at the Master or Doctorate level. These usually focus on a certain area of architectural study. I have not included these degree programs in this book, as this is an initial-entry book.

Bachelor of Architecture (Five years)

The Bachelor of Architecture (B. Arch) program is a program that has been approved by the National Architectural Accrediting Board (NAAB), and has undergone the six-year candidacy period to receive full accreditation. This program is designed for students that are coming straight out of high school or transferring from another Bachelor program (i.e. a college transfer student; anyone who has not yet received their Bachelor degree). This degree is a considered a professional degree, as it is required by most states to be able to receive licensure. These programs are usually five years long and can be very intensive.

Bachelor of Science in Architecture / Master of Architecture (Six Years)

While a Bachelor of Science in Architecture (or any other related architectural area) is not an NAAB-accredited degree, I'm offering this as a path because it is a way to eventually achieve a professional degree. When coupled with the Master of Architecture, it is usually called the four plus two option (four years of undergraduate, and two years of graduate studies). I would offer up this option if you are unable to get into a professional degree program and need some experience in order to prepare to get in. But if you are able to get into a professional degree program on your first try, then I would recommend that path.

Master of Architecture (Three Years; Two Years)

Most schools that offer a Master of Architecture will have two main options for students to achieve a professional degree.

- **Option 1** – This option allows individuals who have a non-architectural degree (a Bachelor of Science/Art in another area of study) to obtain a Master of Architecture. This program is normally three years in length.
- **Option 2** – This option is for students who have a pre-professional degree in architecture. Because of the student's experience with architecture, the program length for this option is usually only two years.

Doctor of Architecture (Seven Years)

The University of Hawaii at Manoa is currently the only NAAB-accredited Doctor of Architecture program. This program consists of 126 undergraduate credits and 90 graduate credits. I will say this, though, once you have your professional degree, it is no longer necessary for you to obtain two professional degrees. So if you have a professional Master of Architecture degree, you may want to look at some PHD architecture programs that focus on a certain area. This program from the University of Hawaii seems to be designed for someone who knows that they just want to go straight through.

What Path to Take

There are a number of different paths that an individual can take to get into architecture school, but I have broken it down into the most common paths. I have also provided the routes that are possible from each area. The starting points are as follows: high school student, transfer student, and graduate student.

High School Student

If you haven't graduated high school yet, you deserve credit because you are taking the initiative to learn early on what needs to be done to get into architecture school. I admire the dedication that you have put forth at an early age. You are responsible and mature, and you deserve to be in architecture school. Don't worry, we'll help get you there. You've already taken care of the hard part, which is staying focused and working hard.

Still in School

I'm breaking the high school portion up into two parts: those still in school and those that have graduated from high school recently. But I want to start with the students who are still in high school because you have an ideal opportunity here; you can still utilize your time in school to create your portfolio. I will go more in-depth a little later with what you should be trying to put into your portfolio, and I will also be explaining in future chapters the various classes that you should be taking. But just know that this is your time to shine and get an edge on your peers who have not had the chance to develop the same opportunities this early on.

So the first thing you need to do is begin studying for the SATs or ACTs, whichever is required for your university of choice. Take the SAT or ACT while still in high school, and write out a timeline that will send you straight into college the same year you graduate high school. Think about which schools you might want to attend, and what interests you in the area of architecture. Start creating projects or pieces for your portfolio. (I will go into more detail a little later on about what you need to do and things that you can pursue to better your options, but for now, just focus on understanding that you are ahead of the game.)

High School Graduate

There are two paths here: good grades and bad grades. If you received good grades in high school (let's say at least above a 3.0; but preferably 3.5 or above), then you can still use the options that trail the end of this subsection. While you won't be able to cash in on some of the advantages that your counterparts have that are still in school, it is not too late for you to get prepped and ready to submit your packet for architecture school. Begin accomplishing the same tasks that were mentioned earlier: SATs, choosing a few schools, creating your portfolio, etc. The only part that may be a little more difficult will be the recommendations, depending on how long you have been out of school, but I will give you tips for that later as well.

For those who graduated high school but received bad grades (below a 3.0 GPA), your path is a little more difficult. It is not impossible to get into architecture school if you try hard, but you will need to accomplish more before you send in your application to architecture school. If you are not too selective with your school choice, you may still be able to take your chances with applying to a program with grades that are at a 2.8 or above. But any lower than that, and I would suggest skipping applying at all.

So what do you do if your grades are too low? You need to begin looking into attending a community college until you are able to get your grades up and be considered a transfer student. I will insert a chapter on community college a little later for those that need information on how to go about taking that route. Community college is not a bad choice, because you will have ample time to work on your portfolio while getting your grades up. If you are going the community college route, then refer to the Transfer

Student section as to what path you need to take once you have your required minimum credits to be considered a transfer student.

Options for High School Students:
• **Bachelor of Architecture (B. Arch) five-year program** • **Bachelor of Science in Architecture four-year program, followed by a two-year program to get M. Arch**

Transfer Student

Congratulations on your interest in making the switch! It's not one that you will regret. First of all, we'll go over what qualifies you as a transfer student and what you can expect when you transfer over. Hopefully you've been researching the classes that you should have been taking in order to prepare for the architecture program. If not, no worries, you will just have a little more courses to take once you have entered the program.

So first things first, you need to figure out if you are actually considered a transfer student by your future school's standards. Most colleges and universities consider an individual a transfer student if he or she has already completed a certain amount of credit hours (24+ semester hours or 36+ quarter hours are usually the standard minimums). If you do not have enough credits yet to be considered a transfer student, then be sure to select classes that are recommended in this book while you try to complete your required minimum credit hours.

For those of you who are transferring programs within a university or college (i.e. transferring from the English department to the Architecture department at the same school), your transition to an architecture program will probably be easier than most. Since you have already been accepted into the school of your choice, you will only have to worry about the other half of the process: the portfolio and the application to the architecture program. If your university/college only offers a four-year architecture program, with a two-year Master of Architecture follow-up, then you may want to take this option. The only reason that you may want to consider this is that when you transfer to another college/university, you may lose credit for some of the classes that you have already taken (some colleges do not fully accept courses offered at other colleges). But if you want to jump straight into a professional degree, then by all means go for it.

If you are at a community college or university, and you want to transfer to another college/university, then you will just follow the processes of someone who is trying to get into a professional degree program. First you will need to start preparing your portfolio and application. Use this time to begin looking for writers for your recommendations as well. You will need to look at each of the schools for the deadlines for the college or university application and also the department application and packet. Later on, I will list in detail what you will need to turn in to each area, but here's a quick overview: SAT scores, high school transcripts, college transcripts, portfolio, university/college application, department application, and recommendations.

Options for Transfer Students:

- Bachelor of Architecture (B. Arch) five-year program
- Bachelor of Science in Architecture four-year program, followed by a two-year program to get M. Arch
- Master of Architecture (M. Arch) three-year program

College Graduate

For those who have already completed their Bachelor degree, this section is for you. There are two areas that are covered here: those that have a Bachelor of Science in Architecture (or other related pre-professional architecture degree) and those that have a Bachelor of Science/Art in something other than architecture. I won't include those that have already received a Bachelor of Architecture (the NAAB-accredited Bachelor degree), because you already know the path to get into architecture Grad School.

As I stated earlier, most NAAB-accredited Master of Architecture programs offer two options to be able to receive your professional architecture degree. Students that have a Bachelor of Science/Art in something other than architecture usually fall under Option 1 (be sure to check on this, as it may vary depending on school). These students will have to attend the university/college for three years to obtain their Master of Architecture degree. This option is a great option for most people who are looking for a program change, as you aren't required to have any prior experience in architecture in order to get into the program.

Option 2 applicants are graduate students who have already received their Bachelor of Science in Architecture (or related pre-professional degree). These students will only have to attend graduate school for two years in order to receive their professional degree. The great thing about this option is that most universities recognize a pre-professional degree from other schools. This allows students to be able to attend different schools so that they are able to receive a broader architectural education.

Options for Graduate Students:

- **Master of Architecture (M. Arch)**
  - Option 1
  - Option 2

ACCREDITED SCHOOLS

Here is a list of the NAAB accredited schools by state (refer to the following codes; Bachelor of Architecture [B. Arch], Master of Architecture [M. Arch], Doctor of Architecture [D. Arch]; those marked with Candidacy status means that they have an approved curriculum outline, but they are still within the 6 year window required to be fully accredited):

You can find a complete list of each architecture school's contact information in the back of this book.

Alabama

- Auburn University (B. Arch)
- Tuskegee University (B. Arch)

Arizona

- Arizona State University (M. Arch)
- Taliesin, Frank Lloyd Wright School of Architecture (M. Arch)
- University of Arizona (B. Arch; *Candidate for* M. Arch)

Arkansas

- University of Arkansas (B. Arch)

California

- Academy of Art University (M. Arch)
- California College of the Arts (B. Arch; M. Arch)

- California Polytechnic State University at San Luis Obispo (B. Arch)
- California State Polytechnic University in Pomona (B. Arch; M. Arch)
- NewSchool of Architecture and Design (B. Arch; M. Arch)
- Southern California Institute of Architecture (B. Arch; M. Arch)
- University of California at Los Angeles (M. Arch)
- University of California at Berkley (M. Arch)
- University of Southern California (B. Arch; M. Arch)
- Woodbury University (B. Arch; *Candidate for* M. Arch)

Colorado

- University of Colorado at Denver (M. Arch)

Connecticut

- University of Hartford (M. Arch)
- Yale University (M. Arch)

District of Columbia (Washington D.C.)

- Howard University (B. Arch)
- The Catholic University of America (M. Arch)

Florida

- Florida A&M University (B. Arch; M. Arch)
- Florida Atlantic University (B. Arch)
- Florida International University (M. Arch)
- University of Florida (M. Arch)
- University of Miami (B. Arch; M. Arch)
- University of South Florida (M. Arch)

Georgia

- Georgia Institute of Technology (M. Arch)
- Savannah College of Art and Design (M. Arch)
- Southern Polytechnic State University (B. Arch)

Hawaii

- University of Hawaii at Manoa (D. Arch)

Idaho

- University of Idaho (M. Arch)

Illinois

- Illinois Institute of Technology (B. Arch; M. Arch)
- Judson University (M. Arch)
- Southern Illinois University at Carbondale (M. Arch)
- The School of the Art Institute of Chicago (M. Arch)
- University of Illinois at Chicago (M. Arch)
- University of Illinois at Urbana-Champaign (M. Arch)

Indiana

- Ball State University (M. Arch)
- University of Notre Dame (B. Arch; M. Arch)

Iowa

- Iowa State University (B. Arch; M. Arch)

Kansas

- Kansas State University (M. Arch)
- University of Kansas (M. Arch)

Kentucky

- University of Kentucky (M. Arch)

Louisiana

- Louisiana State University (B. Arch; M. Arch)
- Louisiana Tech University (M. Arch)
- Southern University and A&M College (B. Arch)
- Tulane University (M. Arch)
- University of Louisiana at Lafayette (B. Arch; M. Arch)

Maryland

- Morgan State University (M. Arch)
- University of Maryland (M. Arch)

Massachusetts

- Boston Architectural College (B. Arch; M. Arch)
- Harvard University (M. Arch)
- Massachusetts College of Art and Design (*Candidate for* M. Arch)
- Massachusetts Institute of Technology (M. Arch)
- Northeastern University (M. Arch)
- University of Massachusetts Amherst (M. Arch)
- Wentworth Institute of Technology (M. Arch)

Michigan

- Andrews University (M. Arch)
- Lawrence Technological University (M. Arch)
- University of Detroit Mercy (M. Arch)
- University of Michigan (M. Arch)

Minnesota

- University of Minnesota (M. Arch)

Mississippi

- Mississippi State University (B. Arch)

Missouri

- Drury University (B. Arch; M. Arch)
- Washington University at St. Louis (M. Arch)

Montana

- Montana State University (M. Arch)

Nebraska

- University of Nebraska (M. Arch)

Nevada

- University of Nevada at Las Vegas (M. Arch)

New Jersey

- New Jersey Institute of Technology (B. Arch; M. Arch)
- Princeton University (M. Arch)

New Mexico

- University of New Mexico (M. Arch)

New York

- Columbia University (M. Arch)
- Cornell University (B. Arch; M. Arch)

- New York Institute of Technology (B. Arch)
- Parsons The New School for Design (M. Arch)
- Pratt Institute (B. Arch; M. Arch)
- Rensselaer Polytechnic Institute (B. Arch; M. Arch)
- Rochester Institute of Technology (*Candidate for* M. Arch)
- Syracuse University (B. Arch; M. Arch)
- The City College of New York (B. Arch; M. Arch)
- The Cooper Union (B. Arch)
- University at Buffalo, The State University of New York (M. Arch)

North Carolina

- North Carolina State University (B. Arch; M. Arch)
- University of North Carolina at Charlotte (B. Arch; M. Arch)

North Dakota

- North Dakota State University (M. Arch)

Ohio

- Kent State University (M. Arch)
- Miami University (M. Arch)
- Ohio State University (M. Arch)
- University of Cincinnati (M. Arch)

Oklahoma

- Oklahoma State University (B. Arch)
- University of Oklahoma (B. Arch; M. Arch)

Oregon

- Portland State University (*Candidate for* M. Arch)

- University of Oregon (B. Arch; M. Arch)

Pennsylvania

- Carnegie Mellon University (B. Arch)
- Drexel University (B. Arch)
- Pennsylvania State University (B. Arch)
- Philadelphia University (B. Arch)
- Temple University (B. Arch; M. Arch)
- University of Pennsylvania (M. Arch)

Rhode Island

- Rhode Island School of Design (B. Arch; M. Arch)
- Roger Williams University (M. Arch)

South Carolina

- Clemson University (M. Arch)

Tennessee

- University of Memphis (*Candidate for* M. Arch)
- University of Tennessee at Knoxville (B. Arch; M. Arch)

Texas

- Prairie View A&M University (M. Arch)
- Rice University (B. Arch; M. Arch)
- Texas A&M University (M. Arch)
- Texas Tech University (M. Arch)
- University of Houston (B. Arch; M. Arch)
- University of Texas at Arlington (M. Arch)
- University of Texas at Austin (B. Arch; M. Arch)
- University of Texas at San Antonio (M. Arch)

Utah

- University of Utah (M. Arch)

Vermont

- Norwich University (M. Arch)

Virginia

- Hampton University (M. Arch)
- University of Virginia (M. Arch)
- Virginia Tech (B. Arch; M. Arch)

Washington

- University of Washington (M. Arch)
- Washington State University (M. Arch)

Wisconsin

- University of Wisconsin at Milwaukee (M. Arch)

CURRICULUM

Bachelor of Architecture

The curriculum for a Bachelor of Architecture tends to be divided into three categories: General, Architectural Subjects, and Design. Each of these areas is usually divided somewhat equally when it comes to required credits (give or take a few classes in each category). That means that about 1/3 of your classes with be in the General category, 1/3 in the Architectural Subjects category, and 1/3 in the Design category. Again, this is just a rough sectioning of each area. Schools offer their own little tweaks to how they provide their curriculum. I will go ahead and break down each of the categories to give you some examples of what to look for.

General

These are usually the general classes that the university requires for you to have a degree. The architecture department has a say in this and oftentimes puts their own stamp on how many of these courses you have to take. Various areas of study within the General category could include: Arts & Letters, Science, Social Science, Multicultural Requirements, Language Requirements, and General Electives.

Arts & Letters, Science, and Social Science usually require about three to four classes in each area. Multicultural requirements, if required at your school, will usually only be about two classes or so. Language requirements can depend upon your department; some universities require two semesters/quarters or anywhere up to two years of Language.

Design

These are the design studios that you will take in architecture school. Basically the design studio is a course where you practice what you have learned in the instructional classes (it is the hands-on portion). Design studio classes usually have a lower student-to-teacher ratio than instructional classes.

This is where you will be spending majority of your time when you get into architecture school. During the semesters when you have a design studio course, you will have your own little space to go to; it's almost like a little office space. (There are times, when you start getting close to project deadlines, in which some students even sleep here.)

Architectural Subjects

This area can include anything that is required within the architecture program: Structural Behavior, Environmental Control Systems, Building Technology, Architectural Analysis, Structural Systems, etc. There are too many courses to list here—and each school varies in what is taught—but your school will have a course list that you can view.

B. Arch Curriculum Example

This is not a hardcopy by any means. Architecture program curriculums change every so often, even within the department. What I'm providing here is a somewhat generalized example of what a Bachelor of Architecture curriculum will look like. This is an accumulation of the top architectural program curriculum.

(Remember that if your school is operating on a quarter system then you will have courses divided between fall, winter, and spring; this is an example of a semester system.)

YEAR 1 - FALL

- Design Studio (6 credit hours)
- Architecture History / Art History (3 credit hours)
- General Course (3 credit hours)
- Mandatory Architectural Subjects (6 credit hours)

Total Credit Hours: 18

YEAR 1 – SPRING

- Design Studio (6 credit hours)
- Architecture History / Art History (3 credit hours)
- General Course (3 credit hours)
- Mandatory Architectural Subjects (6 credit hours)

Total Credit Hours: 18

YEAR 2 – FALL

- Design Studio (6 credit hours)
- General Courses (6 credit hours)
- Mandatory Architectural Subjects (6 credit hours)

Total Credit Hours: 18

YEAR 2 – SPRING

- Design Studio (6 credit hours)
- General Courses (6 credit hours)
- Mandatory Architectural Subjects (6 credit hours)

Total Credit Hours: 18

YEAR 3 – FALL

- Design Studio (6 credit hours)
- General Courses (6 credit hours)
- Mandatory Architectural Subjects (6 credit hours)

Total Credit Hours: 18

YEAR 3 – SPRING

- Design Studio (6 credit hours)
- General Course (3 credit hours)
- Architectural Subject Electives (6 credit hours)

Total Credit Hours: 15

YEAR 4 – FALL

- Design Studio (6 credit hours)
- General Courses (6 credit hours)
- Architectural Subject Electives (6 credit hours)

Total Credit Hours: 18

YEAR 4 – SPRING

- Design Studio (6 credit hours)
- General Courses (6 credit hours)
- Architectural Subject Electives (6 credit hours)

Total Credit Hours: 18

YEAR 5 – FALL

- Design Studio (6 credit hours)
- General Courses (6 credit hours)
- Architectural Subject Elective (3 credit hours)

Total Credit Hours: 15

YEAR 5 – SPRING

- Design Studio Thesis – Final Project (6 credit hours)
- General Courses (6 credit hours)
- Architectural Subject Electives (3 credit hours)

Total Credit Hours: 15

Master of Architecture

The following Master of Architecture programs are listed under two options. Option 1 is for graduate students without a pre-professional Bachelor of Science/Art in Architecture degree. The courses will fall under the following three categories for Option 1 students: General, Architectural Subjects, and Design (please refer to the explanations of each in the Bachelor of Architecture Curriculum section). Since all students entering into the Master of Architecture program already have a Bachelor degree of some form or another, the General course requirements will be in few numbers.

Option 2 is for graduate students who have completed a pre-professional architecture degree. The courses will fall under the following two categories for Option 2 students: Architectural Subjects and Design. Again, this is an accumulation of the top architectural program curriculum. (Remember that if your school is operating on a quarter system then you will have courses divided between fall, winter, and spring; this is an example of a semester system.)

Option 1

YEAR 1 - FALL

- **Design Studio (6 credit hours)**
- **Architecture History / Art History (3 credit hours)**
- **General Course (3 credit hours)**
- **Mandatory Architectural Subjects (6 credit hours)**

Total Credit Hours: 18

YEAR 1 - SPRING

- Design Studio (6 credit hours)
- Architecture History / Art History (3 credit hours)
- General Course (3 credit hours)
- Mandatory Architectural Subjects (6 credit hours)

Total Credit Hours: 18

YEAR 2 - FALL

- Design Studio (6 credit hours)
- General Courses (6 credit hours)
- Mandatory Architectural Subjects (6 credit hours)

Total Credit Hours: 18

YEAR 2 - SPRING

- Design Studio (6 credit hours)
- General Course (3 credit hours)
- Mandatory Architectural Subjects (9 credit hours)

Total Credit Hours: 18

YEAR 2 - FALL

- Design Studio (6 credit hours)
- General Courses (6 credit hours)

- Mandatory Architectural Subjects (6 credit hours)

Total Credit Hours: 18

YEAR 3 - FALL

- Design Studio (6 credit hours)
- General Course (3 credit hours)
- Architectural Subject Electives (6 credit hours)

Total Credit Hours: 15

YEAR 3 - SPRING

- Design Studio (6 credit hours)
- General Course (3 credit hours)
- Mandatory Architectural Subject (3 credit hours)
- Architectural Subject Elective (3 credit hours)

Total Credit Hours: 15

YEAR 4 - FALL

- Design Studio Thesis – Final Project (6 credit hours)
- General Courses (3 credit hours)
- Architectural Subject Electives (3 credit hours)

Total Credit Hours: 12

Option 2

YEAR 1 - FALL

- Design Studio (9 credit hours)
- Mandatory Architectural Subject (3 credit hours)
- Architectural Subject Electives (6 credit hours)

Total Credit Hours: 18

YEAR 1 - SPRING

- Design Studio (9 credit hours)
- Mandatory Architectural Subject (3 credit hours)
- Architectural Subject Electives (6 credit hours)

Total Credit Hours: 18

YEAR 2 - FALL

- Design Studio (9 credit hours)
- Mandatory Architectural Subject (3 credit hours)
- Architectural Subject Electives (6 credit hours)

Total Credit Hours: 18

YEAR 2 - SPRING

- Design Studio (9 credit hours)
- Architectural Subject Electives (9 credit hours)

Total Credit Hours: 18

WHERE TO BEGIN

Deciding which College to Attend

There are many different options out there for a prospective architecture student. Some may prefer ratings. Some may prefer the school's focus in a certain area of design. Others will want to attend purely for the school's location (close to beach, mountains, or home). No matter what your preference, you will at least want to get as much information as you possibly can in what to look for in a university before you apply. Think of it like a job (because that's what it will be for the four to five years you are there... although, more than likely it will be one that you love). I say to think of it like a job because this is your scouting process. You are not just trying to get the job (because we're going to help you make that happen); what you are trying to do is see what the job can offer you! And to do that, you have to see where your interests lie. We're going to view various areas that you should consider before making a decision.

Accreditation

Arguably one of the most important factors to look at when selecting your school is the accreditation. You MUST research to see if the school you want to attend is accredited by the National Architecture Accreditation Board (NAAB). There are only 125 schools (as of the publishing date of this book; there are currently six more schools being reviewed right now) that are accredited by the NAAB. Basically, the NAAB puts their stamp on a college's architecture program to say that it contains the curriculum that will give the student the education needed to eventually become an architect. Why is this important? Well, when you apply for your licensure to become an architect, most states within the United States require you to have attended a NAAB-accredited school/program.

Now, don't be fooled. There are many schools that will try to pitch a Bachelor of Science (B.S.) in Architecture as being a NAAB accredited bachelor degree. This is not the same thing. If it does not have Bachelor of Architecture (B. Arch) or Master of Architecture (M. Arch), then it is not accredited by the NAAB. But, what some schools will do is put you in a Bachelor of Science in Architecture program that rolls straight into an accredited Master of Architecture program; in this case, if you go all the way through to get your M. Arch, then you will have an accredited architecture degree. Just know what you are getting into before you begin. A Bachelor of Science in Architecture (B.S. in Architecture) is a pre-professional architecture degree; a Bachelor of Architecture (B. Arch) is a professional architecture degree.

Location

Location can be important to you for many reasons. One of the biggest reasons for most people choosing location is to be near someone that they know (a girlfriend, boyfriend, family friend, or family member). Just keep in mind, most universities release you during the summer (unless you choose to stay on for summer schooling to try to knock out your degree earlier); you may want to be thinking about some options for what you can do, or what you are willing to do, depending on your acceptance. If you have one school, and one school only, that you are willing to attend, make sure you brace yourself for a possible rejection letter; this is the issue with only applying to one school. But remember that you can always apply again the following year, and that might be a better option for you than attending somewhere other than the one specific university. These are just possibilities to keep in mind.

Another reason for someone choosing location could be that they want to be somewhere where they are artistically stimulated. For me, this would be anywhere near nature (mountains, rivers, beaches, etc.). For others, this might be the city, where they can visually see people interacting with buildings on a massive scale. It will vary from person to person, but it is extremely important to try to attend a university where you will be inspired by your surroundings. If the city depresses you because you love nature, then don't list any schools that are in a major city. If you attend a school in an area where you will not find inspiration, it will show in your work (this is hard for me to say, because an architecture student should be able to find inspiration in the most unlikely of places; but realistically, I would have a hard time finding inspiration in a damp, dark room; know what your limits are, and be realistic).

In-state tuition is another important thing to think about when considering location. In-state tuition is usually offered only to those who are residents of that state. Sometimes going to a school in the state you are from can considerably lower the cost of your degree. In-state tuition is sometimes as much as one-third of the cost of out-of-state tuition for that same school. While this is something to add into consideration, you should not let it be the driving force for your decision. There are many grants and scholarships offered to account for some of the costs, and as we said before, getting into architecture school is the end goal.

Food for Thought:

Some other things to think about when trying to decide on a location for schools:

- Cost of dormitories, apartments, or housing near campus
- Opportunities to find a job in the local area after graduation
- Study abroad (does it offer opportunities to study in other countries for a term)

School Size

School size can play a big part in the decision-making process for some people. You have to figure out whether or not you want to attend a large or small campus. Sometimes the large campuses can offer a good atmosphere feeling like you are pursuing something greater (when everyone around you is studying or trying to achieve their own educational goals). Sometimes a large campus keeps some people from being able to absorb what they need to (i.e. they get distracted from doing work because of all of the activities going on around them). Think about what works for you, and set that as a consideration for your option.

While campus size might not affect certain people, you may want to consider the student to teacher ratios that often comes with campus size. There are going to be generalized classes at a larger university that you just cannot escape (my first architecture class was at least 100+ students, and I'm pretty sure it was closer to 150). At a smaller institution, the student to teacher ratio may not be as large. Generally speaking, the smaller the number of students you have per instructor, the more focus you will receive from that instructor.

Design Focus

Perhaps most that are reading this have some type of basic idea of the various areas of focus in architecture school, but as I have stated before, this book is written as if your interest in architecture began yesterday. Below are some of the areas in which a program might focus. A good architecture school will offer a thorough overview of each area, but some schools are known for their focus in a particular area. The school that I had attended had a deep focus on environmental design, although it also had a sister school not too far away that focused mainly on urban design. Each of the following examples are broken down into raw explanations (many students could speak on each of the areas for hours—or even days—but since you will be doing this when you get to school, we'll just give you the basics).

Urban – When thinking about urban design, skyscrapers usually come to mind, but urban design is much more than just skyscrapers. This area of focus links together architecture and landscape architecture—as well as city planning—to encompass nearly all interactions within the city. If you enjoy seeing the "bigger picture" (i.e. how an individual might react with a space, and how that space might interact with the space beside it, and how those combined spaces interact with yet more spaces) then this might be the area for you). I actually find it very interesting because it goes beyond just the design of a single structure. It is the interaction of a multitude of pieces.

Commercial – In a nutshell, this area focuses on designing for businesses. Many major architecture firms bring in most of their cash from these types of projects. Just a small taste of what commercial design entails is: retail, automotive, offices, and restaurants (the list could go on, but you pretty much get the idea). Some people may or may not enjoy designing at this level. Again, it's all preference.

Residential – Not always where the money is at (but definitely my personal favorite). Residential design is basically designing or restoring homes or portions of a home. Many times, this is the area that starts people off on wanting to become an architect. There is something personal about it, and sometimes *personal* is rewarding.

Environmental – Sustainable architecture (green architecture to some) is not new. What is new is that many schools are finding ways to include this as a focus. Whether it be for environmental concerns, new regulations, or just plain saving money, this area has seen an explosion in recent years. Sustainable architecture can include various features such as renewable energy, water conservation, or energy efficiency (it is an attempt to minimize waste).

Research and Theory – I inserted this into the *Design Focus* category because it is something that should be considered when looking into a school. Most of the top-level schools (Harvard, MIT, Yale, etc.) offer good departmental focus on research and theory. You could say that this area approaches new opportunities not yet considered. This should be something that should be considered if you find a strong interest in this type of thing or decide to pursue a Graduate degree.

This list is not all-inclusive by any means. This is just a basic understanding of *some* of the various areas that should be considered when selecting your school. But, don't get caught up in thinking that you may make a mistake in choosing a school that focuses in something that you may not be interested in later on. I guarantee that at least about 97% of the schools out there offer the opportunity to excel in any of these areas (it's just that some schools offer greater opportunities to study a specific focus). Of course, if you know for a fact that you strictly are going to be designing urban structures and spaces, and have no interest in designing anything else, you may want to research a design specific architecture school.

Food for Thought:
Some other things to think about when trying to decide on the educational focus for schools:
- Knowledge of the faculty (what experience do they bring to the table?)
- The focus of the curriculum (is it well-rounded or does it target a certain area?)
- Opportunities to double major or certify in specific focus

School Rankings

Rankings change too frequently to keep a correct update in here, and I always want to keep you guys and gals as up-to-date as possible. So I'm just going to list 15 of the schools that fluctuate in and out of the top 10, and I'll pass you the link to a book where you can find the most current listing. Remember, these schools are listed alphabetically and not in order of ranking.

> **Side Note:** *If you are finding that you can't sleep at night because you do not know the exact ranking of each school, you'll find that DesignIntelligence offers the most recent collection of rankings for a price. These results are used by*

some of the most popular architecture magazines. http://myschoolofarchitecture.com/best-architecture-schools-book

Undergraduate

- California Polytechnic State University (CalPoly)
- Carnegie Mellon University
- Cornell University
- Iowa State University
- Kansas State University
- Pennsylvania State University
- Pratt Institute
- Rice University
- Rhode Island School of Design
- Syracuse University
- University of Cincinnati
- University of Oregon
- University of Southern California Institute of Architecture
- University of Texas at Austin
- Virginia Polytechnic Institute and State University (Virginia Tech)

Graduate

- Columbia University
- Cornell University
- Harvard University
- Kansas State University
- Massachusetts Institute of Technology

- Rice University
- University of Cincinnati
- University of Michigan
- University of Pennsylvania
- University of Southern California Institute of Architecture
- University of Texas at Austin
- University of Virginia
- Virginia Polytechnic Institute and State University (Virginia Tech)
- Washington University in St. Louis
- Yale University

Side Note: For a complete list of schools that offer architecture, visit: http://www.myschoolofarchitecture.com

Online or Offline

With the rise of unemployment rates, many people are attempting to go back to college for career changing degrees. With this influx of applying students, many universities have started to introduce distance learning options (basically earning your degree strictly from the computer; no classrooms necessary). Now, while I don't believe that online schooling is a bad route for some people (it's the only way some people can earn their degree without having to sacrifice their day job), I do believe that this is an extremely poor choice for someone who wants to go to school for architecture.

Let's examine why online education is a poor choice. The architecture program is such an intensely interactive program that there is no way any university can replicate the same processes online. The majority of your strength of learning your craft will lie within your design studios.

I'll use my first studio project as an example. I mainly just worked on my project at home, only coming back to my studio for classes and when I needed extra supplies. I had thought that working in the comfort of my own home was the most brilliant idea ever. I mean, seriously, it was a quieter atmosphere, and there were more stay-awake beverages to supply my drive to create the best piece that the architecture department had ever seen. So I stayed at home and slaved away over my project, smiling at what I believed was my own ingenious success.

HUGE mistake! I brought my first work to class on the day of presentations and was astonished to see that the piece that I had worked so hard on was nothing in comparison to that of my classmates. The reason? Instead of secluding themselves from the rest of their classmates, they mingled in groups and bounced ideas back and forth; take that, and multiply it by the number of classes (because not only were they mingling within our class, they were also visiting the other studios as well) and you might be able to measure my embarrassment as I stood in front of my design piece. This was the last time I made this mistake; all of my future projects were completed solely in the studio.

Now, with all of this being said, if someone had told me that I absolutely could not get into any architecture school other than an online architecture school, then I'd have probably tried for it, (but that's just because for me it was architecture or nothing). Unless you have no other choice, I wouldn't recommend going this route because you are provided here with the tools to get into a standard architecture school. The only positive thing that I can see from attending an online school is that there is a possibility to take architecture courses until you are accepted into a brick-and-mortar university (if this is the case, ensure that the online college is an accredited college so that you aren't just throwing your money to the wind; by accredited, I do not mean NAAB-accredited, I mean accredited as a college altogether).

Finding Your Fit

Getting into your university of choice can be tricky for any area of study (Psychology, Math, Art History, etc.), let alone architecture. My suggestion to you? Apply to every university that you are remotely interested in. Basically make a list from all of the areas of research that I suggested to you earlier, and then create a list of every university that you would be interested in, all the way down to number 10 (or as far as you can, but at least try to list five schools). This shotgun blast method is normal when applying to any university program. Like I said earlier, it's like applying for a job. You don't just apply to one and wait for them to call you back; you apply to as many as possible, and then select the job you like best out of the ones that returned your request for work.

If you happen to get accepted to all of the schools that you applied to (for one, you're an All Star), politely decline all of the other schools besides the one that you want to attend; I say "politely" because you never know what can happen, and you never want to burn those bridges by saying, "Not going to your school... Cornell's got a better program than you, and you were only fifth on my list." It's better just to decline pleasantly.

If you didn't get accepted to ALL of the school choices, and you only received one or two acceptance letters (not uncommon at all), then you are a prime example of why we do the shotgun blast method. Remember, the end goal here is to get into architecture school, not to get into the number one school in the nation (of course we want to get you the best, but sometimes you have to choose between reapplying the following year and accepting your second, third, or fourth choice). The charts change, and by the time you get out of school, your school could be ranked five or six steps lower. The goal is to get you that experience, while still accomplishing getting you into an environment in which you can thrive artistically (location, design focus, etc.).

Side Note:

STEP 1: SCOUTING – Gather intel on the schools that can offer you what you are looking for in the area of your preference.

STEP 2: PRIORITIZING – Create an ordered list of the schools you would like to attend, with your most preferable school at the top.

STEP 3: SHOTGUN BLAST – Send applications to all of the schools that are on your list (five schools is a good number, but you could go as far as sending applications to 10 schools if you have the time; I wouldn't try for any more than that).

TAKING CLASSES TO PREPARE

Most architecture departments require a similar foundation for required classes. If you have the opportunity to take some of them now to get a head start then be sure to do so. The following list will offer some ideas for what you should be looking into before you attend architecture school. Again, if you do not have the time or money to complete the recommended classes, then do not worry about it. But these are just suggested courses to help you in the future. If you are currently in college and planning to transfer, or if you are still in high school, then this part pertains to you.

What Classes Are They Looking For

Math

Each program varies on what level of math you are required to take, so I would look it up on your school's website. My suggestion is to get as far as you can. If nothing else, complete enough math to allow you to be able to get into Physics, because Physics is a must for the majority of the schools out there. Some people absolutely hate math. To these people I say, "Math is to you as Foreign Language was to me… necessary to get into architecture." In some programs (Art History, etc.), Math can be waived; it is almost never waived for architecture. Depending on your school, you shouldn't have to get into Statistics, and most times you don't even have to get through Calculus. However, if you have the option, you will look better for having upper-level math courses on your transcript.

Algebra and Geometry are required; there is no getting around this. Usually most universities will want to see three math courses, so that means one more advanced math class. Algebra 2 (or its equivalent) is often accepted, and Trigonometry is good too. This subject area is not the "make or break" area, but if you can increase your odds of getting a better look on your packet, it's completely worth it.

Physics

You will be taking this no matter what (at least it seems a part of the curriculum of about 90% of the programs out there). You might as well get it out of the way now. Plus, for all of you math haters out there, this is actually the math that makes sense. My wife absolutely hates math; she always asks, "But why do you need to find x? Who cares what it is equal to?" But now you no longer care about x for the sake of x. You care about x because that is the amount of pressure that your roof will take before blowing off during a strong wind storm. This is the hands-on portion of math. Love it. Learn it.

Art

While Art is not mandatory to get into most architecture schools, you will be required to take it when you are in architecture school. My suggestion, though; don't wait. This is one of the most important pieces of your craft. This will get you to start thinking creatively if you don't already do so, and if you already think creatively, you need to exercise that outside-of-the-box thinking to be able to get the most out of it. Plus, this will be one of the most important classes to get ideas for you portfolio pieces. It is basically mandatory time for portfolio work. And while you are not in Art class, you should be doodling or exercising your drawing skills on a daily basis.

When I was in architecture school, I had a professor that once told our class that we need to be drawing whenever we felt the urge arise, even if it was during class. I thought this was funny at the time because he was basically saying that our artwork and inspiration was more important than anything that our other professors had to teach us. We were architecture students, and nothing else mattered, which is often the thought process of most architecture students. Now I'm not saying for you to do the same thing, because obviously doing this in a constant manner will result in the lowering of your GPA, (and as I've drilled before, GPA is huge when it comes to getting into architecture school). What I am saying is that it is highly important to learn more than you already know. If you have no clue how to draw, classes will help (believe me, it can be taught; I was horrible when I first started). Some people have the innate gift, and maybe you'll be more inclined to use other media when you're actually in architecture school, but drawing is a necessary tool in your early years of school, if not your entire career.

Also, there are many other forms of art than just drawing and painting. Hopefully your school teaches some of these ways. Weaving, photography, graphic design, iron work, wood work, and sculpting are just some of the ways that you can show your creative ability. You'll have more tools in your toolkit for when you get into architecture. I've seen some students do some pretty amazing things with projects because they had taken the time to advance their artistic abilities in other ways, prior to getting into architecture. And the great thing? All of these can offer up possible pieces for your portfolio.

Art History

If your school offers Art History courses, take them. If they offer Art History with a hint of Architectural Art History, take them. Most Architectural History classes will fall under Art History anyways. This is your lifeline to inspiration. If your high school does not offer it, and you cannot take it at the local community college, then just keep it in the back of your mind that you need this in architecture school. I suggest befriending an Art History major. Who knows, you may even decide to Minor in Art History. While I chose Business as my Minor, I had a classmate who had chosen Art History as hers. Her explanation for it when I asked her was, "I want to know my field." That in itself is reason enough to think about adding it as a Minor. Lucky for me that I married an Art History major; I was able to get the scoop on all of the good classes that I knew I would be interested in before signing up for them.

If you have no idea what you might like or draw inspiration from, then be sure to take a class for each area (Asian, Italian, American, etc.). You are going to be required to take generalized Art History classes anyways, but this looks VERY good on your application to the architecture department if you have it ahead of time. It shows that you have an interest in the field that you are going into.

Foreign Language

Ugghh. The dreaded Foreign Language classes. *Note to self: avoid at all costs. Note to future architecture students: Take it. Love it. Learn it.* Despite what I say about this area, it is actually very important for after you get out of school. Some firms may be more inclined to pick you up if you learn a foreign language and are able to speak it fluently. So, why not start early, right? Depending on the university that you want to attend, these classes may not be required for entry into the program. I know that for the school that I went to, we had to have two terms of college level foreign language or two years of high school level foreign language just to get into the program. (And despite all of dislike for foreign language, I've actually taken courses in French, Spanish, and Japanese; it is definitely something good to look into for the future.)

Creative Writing

As I said before, anything that allows you to get your creativity out can only help you. For me, I love creative writing, and I've had some great professors that have inspired me in this department. Actually, my portfolio for architecture school was a mixture of art and creative writing (I would work in quotes from some of my stories that gave me inspiration for an art piece). When you're working on your portfolio, the sky is the limit. The more creativity, the better. Taking a creative writing class is not necessary, but it might help you to tap into some things that you haven't thought about. If nothing else, it might inspire some pieces that go into your portfolio.

English

Inspiration, inspiration, inspiration. If you can be inspired by what is written on the page, you may want to tap into this source. Of course, basic English classes are required for entry into your university of choice, but the upper-level courses (300-400) will often be courses that go more in depth on an era or subject.

General Classes

I know there are many more classes that are offered that could possibly benefit you on your path to the architecture program, but I have just listed the major ones that I believe will help you. If you draw inspiration from any of the other subjects (Psychology, History, Political Science, etc.) then be sure to take them. You are looking to be inspired. Don't stop at my recommendations; search for your own as well. And when you find it, share it!

Side Note: I have listed the classes in order of importance.

1. *Art*
2. *Art History*
3. *Foreign Language (if foreign language is a requirement for getting into your architecture school, then it goes here. If not, then it drops down below math; place it according to your inspiration factor.)*
4. *Physics*
5. *Math*
6. *Creative Writing*
7. *English*
8. *Other General Classes*

UNIVERSITY APPLICATION

This is the initial step you need to take to get into your university of choice. This is more of an administrative portion to your acceptance into the architecture department. You have to apply and be accepted into the university before you can be accepted into the department of architecture (this makes sense if you look at it as: you can be attending a university without having chosen a degree, and then later choose a degree and apply to that department). Unless you don't meet the requirements (and you should, since I helped to show you the way in the earlier chapters), this should be fairly easy. Like I said, it's mainly administrative, so the hardest part will be just trying to round up your transcripts and scores. The following subject areas cover what most universities expect to be turned in at the university level.

SAT

Your SAT scores will not really be a make-or-break part of your application (but this really depends on the school; obviously, in the case of really high-end schools, this will hold more weight). Most universities will provide the average scores for the previous year's accepted applicants, or they will provide the minimum score required to be accepted. In the case of average scores, they are averaged out because not everyone scored high. If you are horrible at taking the SATs, but are a wizard in the classroom, you could offset low scores.

As one of the most widely used standardized tests in the world, the SAT is designed to test the skills that students learn in high school and how well they can apply that knowledge. Colleges use SAT scores in combination with other factors, including high school grade point average, to help determine admission, so it is crucial to understand the test beforehand in order to properly prepare for this crucial test.

For those of you that don't know anything about the SAT, I'll explain. The SAT is broken down into three parts: critical reading, writing, and mathematics. The first section involves reading passages and answering questions about it, as well as sentence completion. The second part involves writing a brief essay as well as multiple-choice questions focused on identifying and fixing grammatical and syntactical errors in writing samples. Finally, the mathematics portion involves answering problems related to probability, statistics, algebra, geometry, and other arithmetic operations. This section is broken down into multiple choice questions as well as a fill-in-the-blank section where students must write the correct answer without a set of choices.

The grading scale of the SAT is a bit complex in that a student's percentile is obtained relative to all other students taking that particular test. First, the student's raw score is calculated, wherein a correct answer to a multiple choice question gives the student one point, while an incorrect answer subtracts a quarter of a point. For the math portion where students must write in the answer, one point is given for correct answers while no points are detracted for incorrect answers.

Once the raw score has been calculated, it is converted into a scaled score, which lets the test makers correct for minor variations in the test, including different difficulty levels for the questions. This score, which can range between 200 and 800, is set to a bell curve, so that the majority of students fall between the 400 and 600 range.

If you're looking for a good score, the best way to practice for the SAT is to do so continuously, both in and out of school; don't cram at the last moment. It is important to understand the format, layout, and timing of the test so you are not surprised by what kinds of questions are being asked or how to answer them. Being familiar with the test format and directions can save valuable time. Lastly, repetition of good test-taking habits will greatly help to improve a student's score.

High School Transcripts

You can usually call up your old high school to find out where you can get your transcripts from. I know that when I requested mine, because I had been out for a while, they were kept at the district records office. Again, your old high school should be able to direct you to these people. Be sure to give yourself enough time, because it can sometimes take a little while to find the transcripts unless you have recently graduated. When I sent in for mine, it was about a three month process. Of course my case was probably the most extreme scenario that can be expected (I had been out of high school for a while, so they had trouble finding my records. When they finally found them, they were just switching all the records to digital, so they were unsure how to go about getting me my records. After much correspondence, we finally got it all worked out); just allow yourself ample time. And remember, your transcript must be an unopened official copy and sent directly to the university.

College Transcripts

If you have any college credits, you will want to send off your college transcripts to the university you are applying to. You can usually request as many copies as you want, but most times the college will charge a fee for each transcript requested. These seem to ship off faster than high school transcripts, but you may still want to give yourself a little cushion by requesting these a little early. Again, these should be unopened official copies that are sent directly to the university.

Essay

Sending in an essay may be a requirement of your university of choice. Be sure to go to their new student application page on their website to see if this is a necessary item. If so, they will usually ask you to write somewhere between a 250 – 500 word essay on your goals, ambitions, and why you want to attend the university. You will want to spend a little bit of time on this one. While it is not as big of a deal as your architecture essay, you still want to take it seriously. Remember, you have to get accepted to the university before you can get accepted to the department of architecture.

While you can include your ambitions to be an architect, I would list your other desires as well. For instance, let's say you chose to attend the university because it was close to home. You could mention that, but it's not going to be a selling point. A better twist on it would be that the university and the surrounding area provide a variety of cultural experiences, as well as ample opportunity for community involvement. Think of things that set you apart from your peers: special interests or life experiences. Think of it as a job interview; it's not only what they can offer you, but what you can offer them. As I stated above, wanting to say that you chose the university because it was close to home isn't the best selling point, but this doesn't mean that you can't use it. Here's how I would write this, if it were my essay:

> *Initially, my interest in the University of Oregon originated from a desire to study in my state of residency. I like to think of myself as practical, and saving money through in-state tuition seems about as practical as you can get. But in my research for the perfect Oregon school, I discovered various qualities of the Eugene* area that expand on my current involvements. The diverse culture, concern for environmental awareness, and engaged community echo my own passions.*

*University of Oregon is located in the city of Eugene

Adding honesty into the paragraph shows that it wasn't written by a robot. Add some honesty and a little character (a little character is good, but you don't want to go overboard). This is what they will want to see. They want to find out who *you* are. Show what inspires you while adding pieces to separate you from your peers. If I were to continue this paragraph, I would transition into how my involvement in Habitat for Humanity led me to develop a sense of urgency to help my local community. I would then follow this with the different programs offered in the University's local area that would allow me to continue my community involvement.

DEPARTMENT OF ARCHITECTURE APPLICATION

I've been at writing this book for a little while now, and I've been itching to get to this part. This is the meat and potatoes of getting into architecture school, and most of the key issues, thoughts, and tips can be found here. I'm excited to write this. "Why?" you might ask. Well, I'm excited for the day that the architecture department receives your amazing portfolio and is blown away by your initial entry. Following these insider tips will help you to stand out amongst your fellow would-be architecture students.

To start off, most architecture departments require some of the same material that is required for your application to the university itself. Examples of this are high school transcripts, SAT scores, and college transcripts (if applicable). Be sure to check with the architecture department of your choice to ensure that you are following the guidelines on what is required for their application process. The reason that you have to turn this in twice (once at the basic university level, and once at the department level) is that most architecture departments want to get an overall idea of the student's capabilities. Be sure to keep this in mind when ordering your transcripts. You will have to have two separate transcripts (sealed) sent to each location.

Recommendations

I always found this to be the most irritating part of the process, mainly because I felt like I didn't have any good references to write a letter of recommendation. The school that I attended required three letters of recommendation, and my first thought was, "I'm going to have trouble finding one person, let alone three." Here's what I suggest to you. If you are still in high school, ask a few of your teachers to write a recommendation for you (be sure to find out if the university you are applying to has a specific template for your recommendation letters first). Be sure to add a variety of teachers, because you don't just want to have all math instructors writing recommendations for you. What you should be looking for is someone who can assess your creative ability as well as your intellectual capability (more specifics to come on what areas they should address).

If you are not currently in high school or college, and you have nobody that you can ask for a good recommendation, you may want to look into taking courses at a local community college to work on your networking. It's time to work on your schmoozing skills. The key here is to take some of the classes with some of the same instructors. You want to get to know your professors. Better yet, get them to know *you*. Two classes with one instructor should be sufficient (and if you weren't able to do that, then one class per instructor will work, but shoot for two).

When choosing people to write recommendations, you want to choose people who also look good on paper. If I have all math instructors writing recommendations for me, I won't have a strong application packet. I would have better odds with all art instructors writing recommendations, but I still wouldn't even go that far. You want to have a variety, but you also want to lean toward the instructors of the courses that I recommended to you earlier in the section of "What Classes Are They Looking For." Obviously, if you have taken an architecture class before, that instructor would be number one, but this will not be the case for

99% of the applicants out there. So what's the perfect line-up? Here's what I would shoot for: one art instructor (to vouch for your artistic ability), one architectural art history instructor (to vouch for your desire and interest in the field), and one physics instructor (to vouch for your intellectual capacity and ability to work with others in labs). This is just the line-up that I would have used, looking back, but you don't have to have something exactly like this. When I turned in my application to the architecture department of my school, I used an art professor, a creative writing professor, and a math professor.

Here's the template I would use when trying to decide on recommendation writers: (1) a person who can judge your creative ability, (2) a person who can judge your work ethic, drive, and ability to succeed in your future endeavors, and (3) a person who can judge your analytical and intellectual capability. Of course, if you know an architect who can write a recommendation for you, then I would drop one of the professors for this recommendation (preferably the person who judges your work ethic, drive, and ability to succeed in future endeavors). If you don't have an architect to pull from your pocket (like the majority of you), then don't stress about it; they are not necessary to the process of getting accepted.

Side Note: Providing your recommender with a copy of your portfolio will help to give them an idea of your talents. Including the essay and experience worksheet will help to seal the deal.

Also, here are some extra food-for-thought areas that your selected recommender might want to take a look at when writing the recommendation letter; insert some of these in there, and you'll be golden:

- Promise of productive scholarship
- Imagination and creative potential
- Ability with graphical or visual expression
- Ability to express self in writing
- Ability to express self orally
- Maturity
- Organizational skills
- Ability to work well with others
- Perseverance or follow-through
- Analytical ability
- Intellectual capability

1) Melissa

2) Maybe spanish (world in ila)

3) Tabitha

Remember: When trying to pick your writers for your recommendation letters, you will want to search for people that can judge you fairly in each of the following areas:

1. *Your creative ability*
2. *Your work ethic, drive, and ability to succeed*
3. *Your analytical and intellectual capability*

Portfolio

If ever there was something that could destroy your possibility of getting into the school of your choice, this is it. The portfolio is the end-all, be-all on your path to architecture school. If you don't get this right then it's game over (at least until the following year). But no pressure. Seriously. I'm going to give you the tips you need to get your packet a first-time go. With all the fuss about the portfolio being the make-or-break piece of your packet, it will actually be your saving grace. Why? Because if you are lacking in every other area (poor past GPA, lack of experience, etc.), an amazing portfolio will pull you from the ground and place you amongst the stars.

Just remember, this is your selling point. Make the portfolio as professional looking as possible. A small binder works, but if you can, try to take it or send it off to a professional printing service that can get it all into one nice little booklet. Just think of it as if your portfolio was your building design, and the application acceptance committee was your client. You are trying to pitch them your piece, so make sure it is as well done as possible. And another thing, MAKE COPIES! Do not send in your portfolio without having made copies. You never know if your portfolio will make it there or make it back your way once it has been reviewed. If your portfolio is to be submitted digitally, then be sure that you review your images before you send them off.

Side Note: *If you are looking for a great book on how to put together a portfolio, I would recommend* **Portfolio Design (Author: Harold Linton).** *This will not only help to give you examples for getting into school, but this is what a lot of students use to put together their portfolio for landing their first job as well. You'll find the link below:*

http://myschoolofarchitecture.com/portfolio-design-book

General Misconceptions

One of the general misconceptions that most applicants have is that the architecture department wants to see how good of an architect you already are. Many people show their superb architecture skills through their advanced plan, elevation, and section drawings. Maybe they've whipped up outstanding floor plans, or perhaps they've designed an entire city on twenty sheets of paper. This is not what architecture departments are looking for. They are not looking for people who already believe they are architects because they can draw up an amazing design for a house. They *are*, however, looking for creative thinkers, people who can step outside of the box to explore that whole other realm. For those that have already been working hard to put together those architecture drawings, I'm sorry, but it's time to change course. Don't scrap what you've done (because it's good practice, and you'll probably get an idea from it for another project later), but you now need to reassess your direction.

Main Media Exercises

Creativity, creativity, creativity. This is what you are looking to show in your portfolio. Most universities will have a general guideline of what they want you to show in your portfolio, at least for main media exercises. Despite these guidelines, you will want to flex on the boundaries that they give you. I'll just throw a few possible main media exercises out there and we can approach them in a creative way. Here are two:

1. *Free hand observation drawing, using a pencil or pen; the drawing must be of a tool.*

   Your first instinct when thinking of a tool might be something like a screwdriver, hammer, saw, or something of that nature. I would suggest to you to look outside of the normal boundaries of what you think a tool is. Let's start to work our brains. Let's say that all of the traditional tools are out of play. Your hand could be a tool. Envision a neatly folded paper being torn down the middle by a pair of hands. The new tool (hands) replaces the traditional tool (scissors); two hands tearing apart a piece of paper is what you would draw.

To show that you can operate on various levels, you might also throw in there that the paper being ripped shows writing that says "Success is unattainable." Or perhaps (for those that like to show off their architectural drawing skills), you could show a building design on the paper that is being torn, as if you were displeased with the design. To add to this, you could now play with the boundaries of the required use of pencil or pen; perhaps you could complete the entire drawing using a "black is white, white is black" effect (coloring in a black background and using the non-colored in portion to show the image you are trying to display).

You can see how far we can take this now, right? We could go on and on. This is the type of stuff that the architecture schools are looking for. Think of an onion (for those that have taken a lot of English courses, you'll get this reference). An onion has many layers that can be peeled back to reveal another layer below.

2. *Self-portrait, using the media of your choice.*

You could go in any direction with this. This is your chance to show off your talents. You can show this through anything: weaving, collage, graphic design, photography, sculpting, iron-working, painting, etc. The sky is the limit (and thinking of sky, perhaps you're a master at Photoshop and want to create your face with an arrangement of clouds). It is all interpretive. Here are some things to think about: (1) How do you view yourself? (2) What medium could you use to show that? (3) How can you peel back the layers?

I'll just play with one idea, just so you can get a feel for a direction that we might go on this. We'll hit on the first question: How do you view yourself? So, I like to think of myself as a little reserved, mysterious, and sometimes dark; at times I feel as though I need to detach from the world, but I also feel as though I can see things that others are unable to see (this covers the first question). The next thing that I need to know is what media I can use for my self-portrait. Well, I love photography, but I also love using Photoshop. For this scenario, we'll say that I'm going to use both. Next in the order of movement: create the first layer, and then start to peel it back.

First, I take a picture of myself in the vertical, full-length mirror. I'm wearing torn jeans and a black hooded sweatshirt, and my head is tilted slightly down. The room is dark, but my entire body is visible in the shot. With this picture, I feel as though I am portraying the reserved side of me. Through this, I have escaped the first layer (which is to show an image of your physical self), and I have passed to the second layer (which is to infuse the physical image with an emotional interpretation). Now I take it a step further and load the image onto my computer and edit it so that my face can't be seen within the hood (this shows yet another side—mystery—while allowing to display my talents in graphic work). To finish, I insert my face from another photograph onto a hanging picture in the background, so that it appears as though I am looking over my own shoulder in the final image (which could be interpreted as something like "I am constantly aware of myself; I am my own critic" or something of the sort).

So in the final piece, I have accomplished a physical self-portrait (although I technically didn't even have to show my face with that last part), an emotional self-portrait (through the "feel" of the image), advertised two media (photography and graphic design), and provided an outside-of-the-box experience (the wide-staring eyes held within the picture frame, looking over the shoulder of a faceless man).

Other Creative Work

The two examples that I previously gave were provided because I mainly just wanted to show the thought process that is needed in order to achieve a well-developed piece. Nearly everything that you put into your portfolio should be layered. There are so many routes that you can go. I would say that one of the best places to start would be to see if the school of your choice has a place where you can view some of the other previously accepted portfolios. I know that my school did, and it helped me tremendously to see the various ways I could go about putting my portfolio together. Like I said before, they want to see creativity. The sky is the limit on this. You don't have to be an amazing artist (I never was, and still am not, although I have progressed).

To show that you don't have to actually draw everything, I'll give you an example of a piece that I had seen in a portfolio sample. In this portfolio, a girl had done a study of one of her artworks. The art piece consisted of rope and trees. Basically, she had gone out into the middle of the woods and strung up rope, one piece at a time (but about fifty pieces total), between twelve trees. She had formed a three-dimensional web of sorts, and then she studied the piece amongst its surroundings. I thought that it was a unique piece because it was unconventional, appealing to look at, and she showed her analytical side through studying the artwork. She also showed her dedication to the architecture program because it was obvious that she had taken a large amount of time to complete it.

My greatest suggestion when it comes to developing your creative work is to not use the same medium more than twice. If all of your drawings are done in pencil, then you are limiting yourself. How is a bland grey on every page of your portfolio going to seem interesting to the people reviewing the application packets? It's not. Instead, try to be different, even if it's only slightly different. On one of the pieces that I did, I recalled my kindergarten days and colored an entire paper in black crayon; I then proceeded to etch my drawing with a straightened paperclip.

> **Side Note:** *At a loss for what media to use? Here's a list of general areas to show your creativity; do not limit yourself to this list, as it should just be used to get you thinking about how wide the scope is in what you use to express your creativity:*

- Sculpture
- Ceramics
- Sketching
- Drawing
- Furniture design
- Painting
- Weaving

- Video
- Web Design
- Photography
- Painting
- Woodworking
- Ironworking
- Clothing design

Essay

Some universities require you to submit an essay. This can vary from anything like asking why you are interested in architecture to what your favorite piece of architecture is. No matter what it is, you should take your time with this. You may want to put together an outline that covers various areas within your essay. If you are more of a creative writer, find ways to introduce that into your writing. If you are more of an analytical writer, be sure to include a small study within your essay (depending on length requirements; your analysis can be something as small as a paragraph). My suggestion? Overall, be honest.

When I wrote my essay, I wrote on Frank Lloyd Wright's Kaufmann House (better known as Fallingwater to some). Of course, I knew that this piece had been overdone because I had seen many entries of accepted portfolios that had been written on the Kaufmann House. But this piece had inspired me so early on that I refused not to write about it in my essay. How did I get around this? I admitted in my essay that I knew that it was something that was overdone, but I stated that I had to pay tribute to the work that had brought me to the point of writing an essay for acceptance into architecture school in the first place. If you find yourself in this place, where you are writing on an overdone piece but can't help it, be sure to also include a less known—but equally complex—piece that can show your growth in your desire to be an architect.

Experience

Some universities want you to include a section in your portfolio that discusses random experience that may relate to architecture (I would say that only one out of five universities ask for this, but I wanted to include it just to give those that need it an idea of what they should be looking to put into this area). Don't worry, this section is not really there to discuss what kind of architecture work you have done before. As I stated before, the program is not looking for what kind of architect you already are, it is looking for highlighted experiences that may show the department a whole-person overview. Here are some of the areas to consider: individual architecture research (what initiative have you taken to learn more about the craft), travel (how much of the world have you seen), community involvement (are you dedicated to improving your local community and its surroundings), previous coursework (architecture, art, art history, etc.), or work experience (architecture firm, CAD, construction, etc.).

It is not a make-or-break item if you don't have a wide variety of these. I'm mainly just giving you an idea now so that you can start thinking about some of this while you pursue your entry into architecture school. You can always volunteer in your community, and one volunteer option that looks good is Habitat for Humanity (you are doing good for your community, but you are also getting hands on experience). Travel is a hard one because most people can't afford to travel outside of the United States, but remember, you're trying to become an architecture student, so put a spin on it, and start road-tripping. Individual research is easy: hit Barnes & Noble and stick your nose in a book. Work experience: Habitat for Humanity, if that's all you can do. Previous coursework: you can't really help this area unless you are one of those that need to go to community college to get your grades up. Don't stress about this part though, because there are always online programs that can be sought out.

> *Side Note:* I am a supporter of Habitat for Humanity. Beside it looking good on a resume and helping to give you a bit of hands-on experience, it is just a great volunteer opportunity. I encourage you to "get your hands dirty." You can go to their website to find options in your local community. http://www.habitat.org

Interview

Lucky for you, most university architecture departments don't require interviews. Some people really enjoy interviews because it is their way to show how passionate they are about the subject matter. Others tend to shy away from interviews because they show how passionate they are through their work, rather than through words. Either way, the university you are trying to apply to should state on their website whether or not they conduct interviews. Interviews are usually done in two different ways: by phone or in person.

Preparing for an interview can be a very stressful experience for many people, especially since a lot can be at stake, so knowing what to expect for an interview and knowing how to prepare can make the difference between getting accepted by the institution and being turned away.

The most important part of any interview is to familiarize yourself with the program. Research what the program is about while making careful notes of any questions you may have, and be prepared to talk about this. Not knowing anything about the school or program can be detrimental, and having even a minor inkling of these things will work greatly in your favor. Come prepared to ask a few questions, as showing curiosity about the school will show the interviewer just how much you want the position.

Have pre-prepared responses to standard interview questions, which may include:

- What interests you about our program, and why do you want to be a part of it?
- What skills or experience do you have that would make you a good candidate?
- How can you contribute to this program?
- What are your goals for the future?

Dressing appropriately for the interview is crucial, but so is being comfortable during the process. That being said, it is important to find equilibrium between proper attire and an adequate comfort level. This may take some time, so do not simply prepare your clothes the night before the interview. Try your outfit on beforehand, and make sure that you'll be comfortable and confident in it during the interview process.

It is important to be punctual—meaning at least early—for an interview, as well as respectful of the interviewer's time. I shouldn't have to say this, but I will. Do not swear, be rude, curse, lie, or whine; simply treat it as a conversation with a school ambassador, and be prepared to ask questions to show your enthusiasm for the department.

Coping with the stress of an impending interview can seem difficult, but if you prepare properly ahead of time there is NO reason to worry. However, it is important to realize that not every interview will be a complete success, but as long as you treat each interview as a learning experience, your odds of being accepted will only increase. Try to relax before the interview, take a few deep breaths, and realize that the more calm and composed you seem the better your odds of impressing the interviewer.

Just remember, if you get accepted to a school that requires an interview, think about the main topics discussed in the "Experience" and "Essay" section of your portfolio. Most questions will be aimed at what drives you, what inspires you, what you feel that you could offer the university, and what you feel the university could offer you (definitely research the focuses of the university before the interview).

> **Side Note:** *Remember that there is a rating factor that universities use in deciding whether an applicant will be an outstanding architecture student. The importance by order is as follows: (1) creative capability, (2) academic performance, and (3) contribution to the program. Think of this as the whole-person view. Creative capability is a must in architecture. Academic performance shows your ability to push through a hard program, and contribution to the program is judged through your life experiences. Shortcomings in one area can be offset by excelling in the other two.*

OTHER THINGS TO THINK ABOUT

Where to Live

There are many different opportunities and perks to living in the various locations on and around the campus area. I've included some basic guidelines for you on this. You will want to select the area depending on what suites your individual needs best. These options are all based on preference, so I'll try to give you as unbiased of a description as possible.

Dorms

If you want to get the full college experience when you start the next phase of your education, living in a college dorm can offer you many benefits. Dorm life keeps you in a central location close to all of the campus action.

Living at a college dorm gives you easy access to the full range of campus services and facilities. If you need assistance with your homework, tutoring centers, helpful students, and professors are only a short walk away from your dorm. The college library, a typical haunt for many students, is well within your reach even in the evening. If you are not in studio yet, and need to find a quiet place to work away from your roommates, you won't have to go far from your dorm to find a good spot on campus.

Dorm life also helps you meet and socialize with your fellow students. You can make friends with other students who live on campus and are in your program. If you have trouble with a particularly difficult concept in a class, you'll be near a full support network of people who you can ask for help at almost any hour of the day. By embracing dorm life, you'll find it easy to attend regular campus activities, including sporting events, social clubs, and more.

If you live in the college dorms, you can save money and time on major necessities. You won't need to buy an expensive parking permit to park close to your class. Instead, you can simply leave your car at the dorm parking lot and walk to class. At some college dorms, you'll find enough nearby stores and restaurants that you won't even have to drive to take care of your other necessities. In addition, some college dorms include regular meals in your bill. You won't need to worry about taking the time to fix your own meals.

Living in college dorms is not without its drawbacks, though. For example, you may end up with a noisy neighbor, or your roommate may have some annoying habits. So be sure to weigh this against the other perks of staying in a dorm and decide what would be best for you.

Alternative On-Campus Housing

Many universities offer their students several on-campus housing options in addition to dorms, including on-campus apartments and on-campus houses. Alternative on-campus housing is usually set aside to help certain types of students to participate in the campus community while maintaining much-need privacy and independence.

As most universities only have a limited amount of residential space, on-campus houses and apartments are only open to students who meet specific guidelines. Often, these on-campus housing options are reserved for married students or for graduate students. Private houses and apartments can help married students to enjoy campus life while still maintaining a family-centric lifestyle at home. On-campus apartments work well for most married couples, but the increased privacy of a house makes this option ideal for couples with children.

Private on-campus housing can help graduate students to stay close to their professors. Graduate students must often make frequent trips to the campus at any hour of the day or night, making on-campus living arrangements an ideal choice. Living in a dorm does not always provide a good work environment for a graduate student, so they usually receive priority as well when applying for on-campus apartments or houses.

The overall price of on-campus apartments and houses is usually much higher than the price of a room in a dorm. However, for certain students, the benefits of these alternative arrangements are well worth the additional cost. Since, as an architecture student you will be spending a lot of your time in the studios, this option is probably the most ideal one for students with families.

Off-Campus Living

For students who don't live near their university, a long commute and the lack of a solid bus route can make off-campus living difficult. Additionally, if you decide to go to school in another state or in a distant city, you will need to need to look for off-campus apartments or houses to rent before you move.

Unlike on-campus dorms, you will have to find an apartment or house and go through the application process on your own. And, unlike on-campus housing, you may have to pay for utilities separately. If you need to split rental costs with a roommate, you may have to spend some time to find an agreeable roommate to share your off-campus living experience.

Although off-campus housing sometimes offers challenges, there are many perks to this type of living environment. First, you will likely have your own bedroom and ample privacy. Even if you need to have a roommate, you can pick your own roommate instead of having one assigned to you. If you take advantage of the off-campus living opportunities near your school, you can still enjoy many of the benefits that on-campus students receive, including access to social events. In many cities, large groups of off-campus apartments and houses have taken root near the universities. These housing options are often populated with students, making them an ideal choice if you want to form relationships with people near your age who also share your educational goals.

Another thing to think about is that choosing to live in off-campus apartments or houses helps prepare you for life after college. While your fellow students who live on campus are only sampling independent living, you will have already accomplished some major milestones in the average adult life. Although students who choose off-campus housing will not enjoy some of the highlights that come from living on campus, these students can still participate in campus life.

Paying for College

In the current, strained economy, a college education is the best path toward acquiring a rewarding and productive career. However, finding a way to pay for college is a dilemma that hinders many from pursuing an advanced degree. There are many options available to those who are willing to look. No one should close the door on a college degree when there are numerous alternatives to fund college. Five of the most popular methods are listed below.

Scholarships

There are a host of interesting scholarship opportunities that are open to individuals, many of which are overlooked. Finaid.org is one excellent source that can point students in the direction of unique scholarships. For example, there are scholarships that are offered for left-handed people, Little People of America, tall people, or for individuals with a particular last name. Believe it or not, Loyola University will give a student a free ride through college, for tuition, if he or she has the last name Zolp and is Catholic! In addition, there are scholarships offered for making a prom dress out of duct tape or making a garment out of wool. While these scholarship opportunities do not apply to everyone, it is worth typing in strange, unusual, or unique scholarships on search engines to find out if any apply to you. Minorities and women may find many opportunities. The finaid.org site also provides a link to sites that are offering free scholarship lotteries. It's all about having the luck of the draw.

Grants

Grants are another popular option to pay for college. Collegegrant.net is an excellent source where individuals can discover ways to fund college through potential grants. Grants are a preferred alternative over loans because they do not need to be paid back. Graduates can leave college without a mountain of debt on their backs. Grant opportunities are listed by field. Grants for minority women, grants for single mothers, and women government grants are other links provided at collegegrant.net. Following these links will require time and more digging. However, a successful discovery is well worth the effort.

Loans

Student loans are another way to pay for college. While many would rather avoid the debt that must be repaid, they are a convenient option. Federal student loan programs generally offer low interest rates and do not have to be repaid until after a student graduates. Students can apply for FAFSA to determine what type of federal aid they are eligible to receive, reducing their overall costs. Even if you are not deciding to accept student loans, I would apply for FAFSA anyways to see what you are eligible for. You can always reject the loan offers later. With some research, it's possible to find the best deals through private loans that are available as well.

Work Study

Many colleges and universities offer work study programs to help students pay for college. Interested students can inquire at the college of their choice about programs that are available. In exchange for a certain number of hours of work on campus, a portion of college expenses will be paid for through their efforts. Usually your school will have a website that offers a list of work study opportunities.

Fund College through Job Reimbursement

There are many jobs that will actually pay for college tuition for those who are interested in pursuing an advanced degree in the field. Many employers are eager to have more qualified staff and are willing to assist monetarily. There may be no cost or the fees may be substantially lower. Now, tuition assistance from an employer might be out of the question for an architecture student, but reimbursement might not be. It would be worth looking into, in case you are unable to fund your entire schooling. Most of the businesses that would offer this kind of opportunity would be bigger firms or corporations.

A CHAPTER FOR THOSE REQUIRING BETTER GRADES

Applying to Community College

If you are starting from the bottom and need to get good grades in order to be considered for architecture school, do *not*—I say again—do *not* stress about getting accepted into community college. Community colleges operate on an entirely different level than universities. They are not there to weed out those who have made previous mistakes. They are there to provide kind of an in-between service—*transitional* you might say. They cater to those who have the desire to improve themselves but might not have the grades, time, or know-how to get into a university. What's this mean for you? Generally speaking, they are extremely helpful in enrolling you into their school.

Application

Many community colleges offer a variety of flexible class schedules. If you decide to take classes at a community college—either to negate your high school grades, or just take some classes that might help you later—you will need to follow certain steps to apply. Although the specific requirements will vary between schools, you can find out what information you need and gather the necessary documents to begin.

Before starting the application process, you'll want to consider your strengths and interests, as well as the amount of time you have to give for studying. It may help to meet with an academic advisor before you apply to discuss the available route to meet your end goal.

First, you will need to request an application. For most schools, a general application requires your background information, education history, and your plans for when you would like to begin. This application is often available online or you may request a paper format. Some colleges require a fee for applying in order to process your paperwork. Depending on what term you would like to begin, you may have a deadline for which you must turn in all required materials.

As part of the application, you will need to supply information about your high school education and whether you received a diploma or your GED. If you took standardized tests while in high school, you may also need to submit copies of your scores. If you have previously attended college at another school, you will need to send copies of your college transcripts. Once the school has received all of the required documents, admissions personnel will look at your materials to determine if you would be a good candidate for a student, and you will then be notified if you have been accepted. The length of time it takes to find out your admission status will vary between schools.

Take advantage of the flexibility and variety that a community college has to offer. You can save money and get some credit toward you architecture degree early on.

Side Note: Getting accepted into a community college is a snap! It's mainly an administrative process. Name, address, etc. Like I said before, you *DO NOT* need to be stressed about applying. You will get in.

Placement Tests

Placement tests are there solely to find out where you need to start at in your coursework. If you are horrible at math, you will start at a lower level. If you are amazing at English (Literature), then you will start at a higher level. The only benefit to scoring high is not having to take so many classes to get where you need to be, but if you aren't at the level that you want to be, don't rush it. Start at the lower level and take your time working your way up; this way, you will know what you are doing once your reach the higher levels.

Community colleges require new students to take placement tests as part of the school's admission policy before registering for classes. Most colleges require testing in the areas of math, reading, and writing. Math tests will cover topics ranging from general arithmetic concepts to college algebra and may include higher skill levels such as trigonometry and calculus. Reading and writing tests will focus on comprehension and essay writing. You should contact your local college to determine what specific tests are administered prior to admission.

If required to take placement tests, there are a number of tools to help students study and prepare for the tests. Each school lists descriptions of the tests on their websites that students can review to get a general idea of the type of material that will be covered in the test. They also provide links to appropriate study material on the Internet, as well as review sheets, sample problems, and writing samples posted directly on their websites. Students can also find free study guides and practice tests online.

Side Note: If you have already taken a higher level of a subject and just need to brush up on it, be sure to talk to someone in the testing lab to get study materials before you take the placement tests. It will save you time and money in the long run.

Meeting with an Advisor

Most community colleges make it mandatory for you to meet with an advisor before you are allowed to register for classes. This is a good thing, in my opinion. An advisor can help you get on the right track to achieving your goals. Be sure to visit the school's website for a list of courses that you are interested in before you go in to see your advisor. Take that list in with you (mirror it to the courses I suggested in earlier chapters), and he or she will let you know what classes you have to take first before you can get into the one you want (you have to take prerequisites sometimes; for example, you have to complete a certain level of math before you can register for Physics). Your advisor will help you plot out a timeline for achieving your goals. If you have never taken any college courses before, be sure to heed what he or she recommends, at least until you have a better understanding of how many courses you can handle per quarter or semester.

Remember: Anything that is not at the 100-level or above will not count when you transfer to a university. Example: MATH 095 is not a college level math course, whereas MATH 111 is. Just remember this when calculating your required transfer credits.

EXPERIENCE WORKSHEET

*Use as a reference for the interview and also to provide to individuals writing your recommendation letters

TRAVEL:

PREVIOUS ARCHITECTURE RELATED COURSEWORK/EXPERIENCE:

INDIVIDUAL ARCHITECTURE RESEARCH:

CONSTRUCTION EXPERIENCE:

COMMUNITY INVOLVEMENT:

VISUAL ART COURSEWORK/TRAINING:

CHECKLISTS

High School Student

All dates vary from school to school, so be sure to check with your school for official dates.

1. Start on creative pieces for portfolio
2. Write essay for Department of Architecture (if applicable)
3. Schedule and take SAT
4. Begin requesting recommendations
   - *Send out requests about 2-4 months prior to architecture application due date, to give your recommenders plenty of time to prepare*
   - *You may also need to remind your recommender of the deadline as it nears*
5. Apply for admission into the University
   - *Deadline is usually somewhere in the late Fall or early Winter of the year prior to your attending date*
     - ✓ Complete your application to the university
     - ✓ Send in your high school transcripts
     - ✓ Send in your SAT scores
     - ✓ Provide an essay (if applicable)
6. Apply for admission into the Department of Architecture
   - *Deadline is usually about a month after turning in the university application*
     - ✓ Complete your application to the Department of Architecture
     - ✓ Send in your high school transcripts
     - ✓ Send in your SAT scores
     - ✓ Make sure recommendations are turned in
     - ✓ Turn in portfolio

7. Fill out your FAFSA
    - *It is available on the 1st of January*
    - *It is key to turn this in early, as you will receive funds before they deplete*

Transfer Student

All dates vary from school to school, so be sure to check with your school for official dates.

1. Start on creative pieces for portfolio
2. Write essay for Department of Architecture (if applicable)
3. Begin requesting recommendations
   - *Send out requests about 2-4 months prior to architecture application due date, to give your recommenders plenty of time to prepare*
   - *You may also need to remind your recommender of the deadline as it nears*
4. Apply for admission into the university
   - *Deadline is usually somewhere in the late Fall or early Winter of the year prior to your attending date*
     - ✓ Complete your application to the university
     - ✓ Send in your high school transcripts
     - ✓ Send in your college transcripts
     - ✓ Send in your SAT scores
     - ✓ Provide an essay (if applicable)
5. Apply for admission into the Department of Architecture
   - *Deadline is usually about a month after turning in the university application*
     - ✓ Complete your application to the Department of Architecture
     - ✓ Send in your high school transcripts
     - ✓ Send in your college transcripts
     - ✓ Send in your SAT scores
     - ✓ Make sure recommendations are turned in
     - ✓ Turn in portfolio
6. Fill out your FAFSA (if you have not already completed this for your current school)

- *It is available on the 1ˢᵗ of January*
- *It is key to turn this in early, as you will receive funds before they deplete*

Graduate Student (No Pre-Professional Degree)

All dates vary from school to school, so be sure to check with your school for official dates.

1. Start on creative pieces for portfolio
2. Write essay for Department of Architecture (if applicable)
3. Schedule and take GRE
4. Begin requesting recommendations
   - *Send out requests about 2-4 months prior to architecture application due date, to give your recommenders plenty of time to prepare*
   - *You may also need to remind your recommender of the deadline as it nears*
5. Apply for admission into the university
   - *Deadline is usually somewhere in the late Fall or early Winter of the year prior to your attending date*
     - ✓ Complete your application to the university
     - ✓ Send in your college transcripts
     - ✓ Send in your GRE scores
     - ✓ Provide an essay (if applicable)
6. Apply for admission into the Department of Architecture
   - *Deadline is usually about a month after turning in the University Application*
     - ✓ Complete your application to the Department of Architecture
     - ✓ Send in your college transcripts
     - ✓ Send in your GRE scores
     - ✓ Make sure recommendations are turned in
     - ✓ Turn in portfolio
7. Fill out your FAFSA
   - *It is available on the 1st of January*

- *It is key to turn this in early, as you will receive funds before they deplete*

For Those Requiring Better Grades

All dates vary from school to school, so be sure to check with your school for official dates.

PHASE 1

1. Fill out your FAFSA
   - *It is available on the 1st of January*
   - *It is key to turn this in early, as you will receive funds before they deplete*
2. Apply to community college
3. Schedule and take placement tests at community college
4. Start on creative pieces for portfolio
5. Write essay for Department of Architecture (if applicable)
6. Schedule and take SAT
7. Begin requesting recommendations
   - *Send out requests about 2-4 months prior to architecture application due date, to give your recommenders plenty of time to prepare*
   - *You may also need to remind your recommender of the deadline as it nears*

PHASE 2

1. Apply for admission into the university
   - *Deadline is usually somewhere in the late Fall or early Winter of the year prior to your attending date*
     - ✓ Complete your application to the university
     - ✓ Send in your high school transcripts
     - ✓ Send in your SAT scores
     - ✓ Provide an essay (if applicable)
2. Apply for admission into the Department of Architecture

- *Deadline is usually about a month after turning in the university application*
  - ✓ Complete your application to the Department of Architecture
  - ✓ Send in your high school transcripts
  - ✓ Send in your SAT scores
  - ✓ Make sure recommendations are turned in
  - ✓ Turn in portfolio

SCHOOL CONTACT INFORMATION

For more information on the various schools, visit:
http://myschoolofarchitecture.com

ALABAMA:

Auburn University

    Degree:

    Bachelor of Architecture

    Location:

    Architecture, Planning and Landscape Architecture
    104 Dudley Hall – Auburn University
    Auburn, AL 36849

    Phone:
    (334) 844-4367

    Email:
    admissions@auburn.edu

Tuskegee University
Degree:
Bachelor of Architecture

Location:
Robert R Taylor School of Architecture and Construction Science
Department of Architecture
Wilcox Building C, Room 115 -Tuskegee University
Tuskegee, AL 36088

Phone:
(334) 727-8329

Email:
bradshawc@mytu.tuskegee.edu

ARIZONA:

Arizona State University
Degree:
Master of Architecture

Location:
ASU Herberger Institute for Design and the Arts
The Design School
PO Box 871605
Tempe, AZ 85287

Phone:
(480) 965-0968

Email:
thomas.hartman@asu.edu

Taliesin, Frank Lloyd Wright School of Architecture
    Degree:
    Master of Architecture

    Location:
    Taliesin, Frank Lloyd Wright School of Architecture
    Taliesin West
    PO Box 4430
    Scottsdale, AZ 85261

    Phone:
    (480) 627-5345

    Email:
    ndeporter@taliesin.edu

University of Arizona
    Degree:
    Bachelor of Architecture;
    Candidate for Master of Architecture

    Location:
    College of Architecture & Planning & Landscape
    Architecture
    PO Box 210075
    Tucson, AZ 85721

    Phone:
    (520) 621-6751

ARKANSAS:

University of Arkansas
    Degree:
    Bachelor of Architecture

    Location:
    Fay Jones School of Architecture
    112 W Center St, Suite 700
    Fayetteville, AR 72701

    Phone:
    (479) 575-4945

CALIFORNIA:

Academy of Art University
    Degree:
    Master of Architecture

    Location:
    Academy of Art University
    PO Box 193844
    San Francisco, CA 94119

    Phone:
    (800) 544-2787

California College of the Arts

> **Degree:**
> Bachelor of Architecture;
> Master of Architecture

> **Location:**
> California College of the Arts
> School of Architecture
> 1111 Eighth Street
> San Francisco, CA 94107

> **Phone:**
> (415) 703-9500

> **Email:**
> enroll@cca.edu

California Polytechnic State University at San Luis Obispo

> **Degree:**
> Bachelor of Architecture

> **Location:**
> Architecture Department
> California Polytechnic State University
> San Luis Obispo, CA 93407

> **Phone:**
> (805) 756-1316

> **Email:**
> architecture@calpoly.edu

California State Polytechnic University in Pomona

Degree:

Bachelor of Architecture;

Master of Architecture

Location:

College of Environmental Design

California State Polytechnic University, Pomona

3801 West Temple Avenue, Bldg 7

Pomona, CA 91768

Phone:

(909) 869-2683

Email:

rksanchez@csupomona.edu

NewSchool of Architecture and Design

Degree:

Bachelor of Architecture;

Master of Architecture

Location:

NewSchool of Architecture and Design

1249 F Street

San Diego, CA 92101

Phone:

(800) 490-7081

Email:

NSADinquiries@newschoolarch.edu

Southern California Institute of Architecture

Degree:

Bachelor of Architecture;

Master of Architecture

Location:

Southern California Institute of Architecture

960 East 3rd Street

Los Angeles, CA 90013

Phone:

213-356-5320

Email:

admissions@sciarc.edu

University of California at Los Angeles

Degree:

Master of Architecture

Location:

UCLA Department of Architecture & Urban Design

Box 951467

Los Angeles, CA 90095

Phone:

310-825-7857

Email:

admissions@aud.ucla.edu

University of California at Berkley

   Degree:

   Master of Architecture

   Location:

   University of California, Berkeley
   232 Wurster Hall #1800
   Berkeley, CA 94720

   Phone:

   (510) 642-4942

   Email:

   archgrad@berkeley.edu

University of Southern California

   Degree:

   Bachelor of Architecture;
   Master of Architecture

   Location:

   USC, School of Architecture
   Watt Hall, Suite 204
   Los Angeles, CA 90089

   Phone:

   (213) 740-2723

   Email:

   archgrad@usc.edu

Woodbury University

Degree:
Bachelor of Architecture;
Candidate for Master of Architecture

Location:
Woodbury University
7500 Glenoaks Blvd.
Burbank, CA 91510

Phone:
(818) 252-5133

Email:
Cesar.magallon@woodbury.edu

COLORADO:

University of Colorado at Denver

Degree:
Master of Architecture

Location:
College of Architecture and Planning
University of Colorado Denver
Campus Box 126, PO Box 173364
Denver, CO 80217

Phone:
(303) 556-3382

Email:
cap@ucdenver.edu

CONNECTICUT:

University of Hartford

Degree:

Master of Architecture

Location:

University of Hartford
United Technologies Hall 209C
200 Bloomfield Avenue
West Hartford, CT 06117

Phone:

(860) 768-4446

Email:

kcofiell@hartford.edu

Yale University

Degree:

Master of Architecture

Location:

Yale School of Architecture
180 York Street
New Haven, CT 06511

Phone:

(203) 432-2288

Email:

gradarch.admissions@yale.edu

DISTRICT OF COLUMBIA (WASHINGTON D.C.):

Howard University
    Degree:
    Bachelor of Architecture

    Location:
    Department of Architecture
    College of Engineering, Architecture and Computer Sciences
    Howard University - 2366 Sixth Street NW
    Washington, DC 20059

    Phone:
    (202) 806-7424

    Email:
    ceacs@howard.edu

The Catholic University of America
    Degree:
    Master of Architecture

    Location:
    The Catholic University of America
    Office of University Admissions
    620 Michigan Ave, NE
    Washington, DC 20064

    Phone:
    (202) 319-5305

    Email:
    cua-admissions@cua.edu

FLORIDA:

Florida A&M University

> **Degree:**
> Bachelor of Architecture;
> Master of Architecture

> **Location:**
> Florida A&M University
> School of Architecture
> Walter Smith Architecture Building
> 1938 S. Martin Luther King, Jr. Blvd.
> Tallahassee, FL 32307

> **Phone:**
> (850) 599-3244

Florida Atlantic University

> **Degree:**
> Bachelor of Architecture

> **Location:**
> Florida Atlantic University
> School of Architecture
> FAU/BCC Higher Education Complex
> 111 East Las Olas Boulevard
> Fort Lauderdale, FL 33301

> **Phone:**
> (954) 762-5654

> **Email:**
> architecture@fau.edu

Florida International University
>**Degree:**
>
>Master of Architecture
>
>**Location:**
>
>School of Architecture
>Paul L. Cejas School of Architecture Building
>Modesto Maidique Campus
>11200 SW 8th Street - PCA 272
>Miami, FL 33174
>
>**Phone:**
>(305) 348-7500
>
>**Email:**
>soa@fiu.edu

University of Florida
>**Degree:**
>
>Master of Architecture
>
>**Location:**
>
>UF School of Architecture
>POB 115702
>Gainesville FL 32611-5702
>
>**Phone:**
>(352) 392-0205
>
>**Email:**
>nmclark@ufl.edu

University of Miami

> **Degree:**
>
> Bachelor of Architecture;
>
> Master of Architecture
>
> **Location:**
>
> University of Miami School of Architecture
>
> 1223 Dickinson Drive
>
> Coral Gables, FL 33146
>
> **Phone:**
>
> (305) 284-3731
>
> **Email:**
>
> architecture@miami.edu

University of South Florida

> **Degree:**
>
> Master of Architecture
>
> **Location:**
>
> USF School of Architecture and Community Design
>
> 4202 E. Fowler Avenue, HMS 301
>
> Tampa, FL 33620
>
> **Phone:**
>
> (813) 974-4031
>
> **Email:**
>
> info@arch.usf.edu

GEORGIA:

Georgia Institute of Technology
> **Degree:**
> Master of Architecture
>
> **Location:**
> Georgia Tech College of Architecture
> 245 4th St. NW
> Atlanta, GA., 30332
>
> **Phone:**
> (404) 894-3880

Savannah College of Art and Design
> **Degree:**
> Master of Architecture
>
> **Location:**
> SCAD Admission Department
> 22 E Lathrop Ave
> Savannah, GA 31415 USA
>
> **Phone:**
> (912) 525-5100
>
> **Email:**
> admission@scad.edu

Southern Polytechnic State University

Degree:

Bachelor of Architecture

Location:

SPSU Architecture

Building N

1100 South Marietta Pkwy

Marietta, GA 30060

Phone:

(678)915-7253

Email:

admissions@spsu.edu

HAWAII:

University of Hawaii at Manoa

Degree:

Doctor of Architecture

Location:

University of Hawaii at Manoa

School of Architecture

2410 Campus Road

Honolulu, HI 96822

Phone:

(808) 956-7225

Email:

arch@hawaii.edu

IDAHO:

University of Idaho
    Degree:
    Master of Architecture

    Location:
    College of Art and Architecture
    University of Idaho
    875 Perimeter Drive MS 2451
    Moscow, ID 83844

    Phone:
    (208) 885-6781

    Email:
    arch@uidaho.edu

ILLINOIS:

Illinois Institute of Technology
    Degree:
    Bachelor of Architecture;
    Master of Architecture

    Location:
    IIT College of Architecture
    3360 S State St
    Chicago, IL 60616

    Phone:
    (312) 567-3230

    Email:
    arch@iit.edu

Judson University

Degree:

Master of Architecture

Location:

Judson University
1151 N. State Street
Elgin, IL 60123

Phone:

(847) 628-2510

Southern Illinois University at Carbondale

Degree:

Master of Architecture

Location:

SIUC School of Architecture MC 4337
410 Quigley Hall
875 South Normal Street
Carbondale IL 62901

Phone:

(618) 453-3734

Email:

jdobbins@siu.edu

The School of the Art Institute of Chicago

    Degree:

    Master of Architecture

    Location:

    School of the Art Institute of Chicago

    36 South Wabash

    Chicago, IL 60603

    Phone:

    (312) 629-6100

    Email:

    admiss@saic.edu

University of Illinois at Chicago

    Degree:

    Master of Architecture

    Location:

    School of Architecture MC 030

    Room 3100 Art & Architecture Building

    845 West Harrison Street

    Chicago, IL 60607

    Phone:

    (312) 996-3335

    Email:

    arch@uic.edu

University of Illinois at Urbana-Champaign

Degree:
Master of Architecture

Location:
School of Architecture
117 Temple Hoyne Buell Hall
611 Lorado Taft Drive, MC-621
Champaign, IL 61820

Phone:
(217) 244-4723

Email:
arch-grad@uiuc.edu

INDIANA:

Ball State University

Degree:
Master of Architecture

Location:
College of Architecture & Planning
Architecture Building, Room 104
Ball State University
Muncie, IN 47306

Phone:
(765) 285-5859

Email:
cap@bsu.edu

University of Notre Dame

 Degree:

 Bachelor of Architecture;

 Master of Architecture

 Location:

 School of Architecture

 110 Bond Hall

 Notre Dame, IN 46556

 Phone:

 (574) 631-6137

 Email:

 arch@nd.edu

IOWA:

Iowa State University

 Degree:

 Bachelor of Architecture;

 Master of Architecture

 Location:

 Department of Architecture

 146 College of Design

 Iowa State University

 Ames, IA 50011

 Phone:

 (515) 294-4717

 Email:

 cjjohn@iastate.edu

KANSAS:

Kansas State University
Degree:
Master of Architecture

Location:
College of Architecture, Planning, and Design
Kansas State University
115 Seaton Hall
Manhattan KS 66506

Phone:
(785) 532-5950

University of Kansas
Degree:
Master of Architecture

Location:
The University of Kansas
205 Marvin Hall
Lawrence, KS 66045

Phone:
(785) 864-3167

KENTUCKY:

University of Kentucky
    Degree:
    Master of Architecture

    Location:
    University of Kentucky - College of Design
    117 Pence Hall
    Lexington, KY 40506

    Phone:
    (859) 257-7617

    Email:
    codstudentservices@uky.edu

LOUISIANA:

Louisiana State University
    Degree:
    Bachelor of Architecture;
    Master of Architecture

    Location:
    School of Architecture
    136 Atkinson Hall
    Louisiana State University
    Baton Rouge, LA 70803

    Phone:
    (225) 578-6885

    Email:
    sarch@lsu.edu

Louisiana Tech University

Degree:
Master of Architecture

Location:
School of Architecture
Louisiana Tech University
Box 3147
Ruston, LA 71272

Phone:
(318) 257-2816

Email:
puljak@latech.edu

Southern University and A&M College

Degree:
Bachelor of Architecture

Location:
Southern University and A&M College
School of Architecture
Baton Rouge, LA 70813

Phone:
(225) 771-4500

Tulane University

> **Degree:**
>
> Master of Architecture
>
> **Location:**
>
> Tulane University
> Richardson Memorial Hall
> 6823 St Charles Ave
> New Orleans, LA 70118
>
> **Phone:**
> (504) 865-5389
>
> **Email:**
> tsarch@tulane.edu

University of Louisiana at Lafayette

> **Degree:**
>
> Bachelor of Architecture;
> Master of Architecture
>
> **Location:**
>
> School of Architecture & Design
> University of Louisiana at Lafayette
> 421 East Lewis Street
> Lafayette, LA 70503
>
> **Phone:**
> (337) 482-6225
>
> **Email:**
> arch@louisiana.edu

MARYLAND:

Morgan State University

> **Degree:**
> Master of Architecture

> **Location:**
> Morgan State University
> 1700 East Cold Spring Lane
> Baltimore, MD 21251

> **Phone:**
> (443) 885-3225

> **Email:**
> sap@morgan.edu

University of Maryland

> **Degree:**
> Master of Architecture

> **Location:**
> University of Maryland
> School of Architecture, Planning & Preservation
> Building 145
> College Park, MD 20742

> **Phone:**
> (301) 405-8000

> **Email:**
> arcinfo@umd.edu

MASSACHUSETTS:

Boston Architectural College
>**Degree:**
>Bachelor of Architecture;
>Master of Architecture
>
>**Location:**
>Boston Architectural College
>320 Newbury Street
>Boston, MA 02115
>
>**Phone:**
>(617) 585-0100
>
>**Email:**
>admissions@the-bac.edu

Harvard University
>**Degree:**
>Master of Architecture
>
>**Location:**
>Graduate School of Design
>Harvard University
>48 Quincy
>Gund Hall
>Cambridge, MA 02138
>
>**Phone:**
>(617) 495-1000

Massachusetts College of Art and Design

Degree:
Candidate for Master of Architecture

Location:
Massachusetts College of Art and Design
621 Huntington Ave
Boston, MA 02115

Phone:
(617) 879-7000

Massachusetts Institute of Technology

Degree:
Master of Architecture

Location:
MIT Department of Architecture
77 Massachusetts Avenue
Room 7-337
Cambridge, MA 02139

Phone:
(617) 253-7791

Email:
arch@mit.edu

Northeastern University

Degree:

Master of Architecture

Location:

School of Architecture
Northeastern University
151 Ryder Hall
360 Huntington Ave
Boston, MA 02115

Phone:

(617) 373-4637

Email:

architecture@neu.edu

University of Massachusetts Amherst

Degree:

Master of Architecture

Location:

Architecture & Design Program
Department of Art, Architecture & Art History
University of Massachusetts
Fine Arts Center, Room 457
151 Presidents Drive
Amherst, MA 01003

Phone:

(413) 577-0943

Email:

architecture@art.umass.edu

Wentworth Institute of Technology

Degree:

Master of Architecture

Location:

Department of Architecture
Annex North, Room 100
550 Huntington Avenue
Boston, MA 02115

Phone:

(617) 989-4450

Email:

architecture@wit.edu

MICHIGAN:

Andrews University

Degree:

Master of Architecture

Location:

School of Architecture
Architecture Building
Andrews University
Berrien Springs, MI 49104

Phone:

(269) 471-6003

Email:

architecture@andrews.edu

Lawrence Technological University

    Degree:

Master of Architecture

    Location:

Lawrence Technological University
Architecture & Design
Architecture Bldg., A116
21000 West Ten Mile Road
Southfield, MI 48075

    Phone:
(248)204-2800

    Email:
archdean@ltu.edu

University of Detroit Mercy

    Degree:

Master of Architecture

    Location:

School of Architecture
University of Detroit Mercy
4001 West McNichols Road
Detroit, MI 48221

    Phone:
(313) 993-1532

University of Michigan

Degree:

Master of Architecture

Location:

Taubman College of Architecture and Urban Planning
University of Michigan
2000 Bonisteel Boulevard
Ann Arbor, MI 48109

Phone:

(734) 764-130

Email:

taubmancollegestudentservices@umich.edu

MINNESOTA:

University of Minnesota

Degree:

Master of Architecture

Location:

UMN School of Architecture
Rapson Hall - Room 145
89 Church Street
Minneapolis, MN 55455

Phone:

(612) 624-7866

Email:

archinfo@umn.edu

MISSISSIPPI:

Mississippi State University
    Degree:
    Bachelor of Architecture

    Location:

    School of Architecture
    899 Collegeview St
    240 Giles Hall Post Office Box AQ
    Mississippi State, MS 39762

    Phone:
    (662) 325-2202

MISSOURI:

Drury University
    Degree:
    Bachelor of Architecture;
    Master of Architecture

    Location:
    Drury University
    900 North Benton Avenue
    Springfield, MO 65802

    Phone:
    (800) 922-2274

Washington University at St. Louis

Degree:
Master of Architecture

Location:
Sam Fox School of Design & Visual Arts
Washington University in St. Louis
Campus Box 1213
One Brookings Drive
St. Louis, MO 63130

Phone:
(314) 935-6500

MONTANA:

Montana State University

Degree:
Master of Architecture

Location:
School of Architecture
Montana State University
160 Cheever Hall
Bozeman, MT 59717

Phone:
(406) 994-4255

Email:
architect@montana.edu

NEBRASKA:

University of Nebraska
    Degree:
    Master of Architecture

    Location:
    College of Architecture
    Dean's Office
    Rm. 210 Architecture Hall
    P.O. Box 880106
    Lincoln, NE 68588

    Phone:
    (402) 472-9212

    Email:
    jenna.hilligoss@unl.edu

NEVADA:

University of Nevada at Las Vegas
    Degree:
    Master of Architecture

    Location:
    University of Nevada at Las Vegas
    4505 South Maryland Parkway
    Las Vegas, NV 89154

    Phone:
    (702) 895-3031

NEW JERSEY:

New Jersey Institute of Technology
> **Degree:**
> Bachelor of Architecture;
> Master of Architecture

> **Location:**
> School of Art & Design
> College of Architecture and Design
> New Jersey Institute of Technology
> University Heights
> Newark, NJ 07102

> **Phone:**
> (973) 642-7576

> **Email:**
> amada@njit.edu

Princeton University
> **Degree:**
> Master of Architecture

> **Location:**
> Princeton University
> School of Architecture
> Princeton, NJ 08544

> **Phone:**
> (609) 258-3641

> **Email:**
> soa@princeton.edu

NEW MEXICO:

University of New Mexico
>   **Degree:**
>   Master of Architecture

>   **Location:**
>   School of Architecture and Planning
>   MSC 04-2530
>   George Pearl Hall
>   1 University of New Mexico
>   Albuquerque, NM 87131

>   **Phone:**
>   (505) 277-0111

>   **Email:**
>   saap@unm.edu

NEW YORK:

Columbia University
>   **Degree:**
>   Master of Architecture

>   **Location:**
>   Graduate School of Architecture, Planning and Preservation
>   Columbia University
>   400 Avery Hall
>   1172 Amsterdam Avenue
>   New York, NY 10027

>   **Phone:**
>   (212) 854-3414

Cornell University
> **Degree:**
> Bachelor of Architecture;
> Master of Architecture
>
> **Location:**
> Department of Architecture
> College of Architecture, Art, and Planning
> Cornell University
> 139 E. Sibley Hall
> Ithaca, NY 14853
>
> **Phone:**
> (607) 255-5236
>
> **Email:**
> cuarch@cornell.edu

New York Institute of Technology
> **Degree:**
> Bachelor of Architecture
>
> **Location:**
> School of Architecture and Design
> Education Hall, rm. 123
> Old Westbury, NY 11568
>
> **Phone:**
> (516) 686-7659
>
> **Email:**
> nyitarch@nyit.edu

Parsons The New School for Design

    Degree:

    Master of Architecture

    Location:

    Parsons The New School for Design
    Office of Admission
    72 Fifth Avenue, 2nd floor
    New York, NY 10011

    Phone:
    (212) 229-8989

    Email:
    thinkparsons@newschool.edu

Pratt Institute

    Degree:

    Bachelor of Architecture;
    Master of Architecture

    Location:

    Office of the Dean
    School of Architecture, Higgins Hall
    61 St. James Place
    Brooklyn, NY 11238

    Phone:
    (718) 399-4327

    Email:
    admissions@pratt.edu

Rensselaer Polytechnic Institute

Degree:

Bachelor of Architecture;
Master of Architecture

Location:

Rensselaer Polytechnic Institute
School of Architecture
110 8th Street - Greene Building
Troy, NY 12180

Phone:
(518) 276-6466

Rochester Institute of Technology

Degree:

Candidate for Master of Architecture

Location:

Golisano Institute for Sustainability
Rochester Institute of Technology
111 Lomb Memorial Drive
Rochester, NY 14623

Phone:
(585) 475-4990

Email:
info@sustainability.rit.edu

Syracuse University

> **Degree:**
>
> Bachelor of Architecture;
>
> Master of Architecture
>
> **Location:**
>
> School of Architecture
>
> Syracuse University
>
> 201 Slocum Hall
>
> Syracuse, NY 13244
>
> **Phone:**
>
> (315) 443-2256

The City College of New York

> **Degree:**
>
> Bachelor of Architecture;
>
> Master of Architecture
>
> **Location:**
>
> The Bernard and Anne Spitzer School of Architecture
>
> 141 Convent Avenue
>
> New York, NY 10031
>
> **Phone:**
>
> (212) 650-7118
>
> **Email:**
>
> architecture@ccny.cuny.edu

The Cooper Union

> **Degree:**
>
> Bachelor of Architecture
>
> **Location:**
>
> The Cooper Union
> Admissions Department
> 30 Cooper Square, Third Floor
> New York, NY 10003
>
> **Phone:**
> (212) 353-4100

University at Buffalo, The State University of New York

> **Degree:**
>
> Master of Architecture
>
> **Location:**
>
> Department of Architecture
> 114 Diefendorf Hall
> Buffalo, NY 14214
>
> **Phone:**
> (716) 829-3473
>
> **Email:**
> ap-architecture@buffalo.edu

NORTH CAROLINA:

North Carolina State University
>   **Degree:**
>   Bachelor of Architecture;
>   Master of Architecture
>
>   **Location:**
>   College of Design - NC State University
>   Campus Box 7701
>   Raleigh, NC 27695
>
>   **Phone:**
>   (919) 515-8306
>
>   **Email:**
>   design@ncsu.edu

University of North Carolina at Charlotte
>   **Degree:**
>   Bachelor of Architecture;
>   Master of Architecture
>
>   **Location:**
>   School of Architecture
>   University of North Carolina at Charlotte
>   9201 University City Boulevard
>   Charlotte, NC 28223
>
>   **Phone:**
>   (704) 687-0102
>
>   **Email:**
>   wrroosen@uncc.edu

NORTH DAKOTA:

North Dakota State University
   Degree:
   Master of Architecture

   Location:
   NDSU Department of Architecture & Landscape
   Architecture
   650 NP Avenue
   Fargo, ND 58102

   Phone:
   (701) 231-6151

   Email:
   ndsu.ala@ndsu.edu

OHIO:

Kent State University
   Degree:
   Master of Architecture

   Location:
   College of Architecture
   & Environmental Design
   201 Taylor Hall,
   Kent State University
   Kent, OH 44242

   Phone:
   (330) 672-0921

   Email:
   mjgear@kent.edu

Miami University

> **Degree:**
>
> Master of Architecture
>
> **Location:**
>
> School of Architecture & Interior Design
> Miami University
> 101 Alumni Hall
> Oxford, OH 45056
>
> **Phone:**
> (513) 529.7210
>
> **Email:**
> arcid@muohio.edu

Ohio State University

> **Degree:**
>
> Master of Architecture
>
> **Location:**
>
> Ohio State University
> Knowlton School of Architecture
> 275 West Woodruff Avenue
> Columbus, OH 43210
>
> **Phone:**
> (614) 292-1012

University of Cincinnati

Degree:
Master of Architecture

Location:
College of DAAP
5470 Aronoff Center
PO Box 210016
Cincinnati, OH 45221

Phone:
(513) 556-1376

Email:
daap-admissions@uc.edu

OKLAHOMA:

Oklahoma State University

Degree:
Bachelor of Architecture

Location:
School of Architecture
101 Donald W Reynolds School of Architecture Building
Oklahoma State University
Stillwater, OK 74078

Phone:
(405) 744-6043

Email:
suzanne.bilbeisi@okstate.edu

University of Oklahoma

>**Degree:**
>
>Bachelor of Architecture;
>
>Master of Architecture
>
>**Location:**
>
>College of Architecture
>University of Oklahoma
>830 Van Vleet Oval
>Norman, OK 73019
>
>**Phone:**
>(405) 325-2444
>
>**Email:**
>coa-communications@ou.edu

OREGON:

Portland State University

>**Degree:**
>
>*Candidate for* Master of Architecture
>
>**Location:**
>
>Department of Architecture – Portland State University
>Shattuck Hall, Suite 235
>P.O. Box 751
>Portland, OR 97207
>
>**Phone:**
>(503) 725-8405
>
>**Email:**
>architecture@pdx.edu

University of Oregon

    Degree:

    Bachelor of Architecture;
    Master of Architecture

    Location:

    University of Oregon
    School of Architecture and Allied Arts
    210 Lawrence Hall
    1206 University of Oregon
    Eugene, OR 97403

    Phone:
    (541) 346-3656

    Email:
    archinfo@uoregon.edu

PENNSYLVANIA:

Carnegie Mellon University

    Degree:
    Bachelor of Architecture

    Location:
    School of Architecture
    201 College of Fine Arts
    Pittsburgh, PA 15213

    Phone:
    (412) 268-2354

Drexel University

> **Degree:**
> Bachelor of Architecture

> **Location:**
> Drexel University
> 3141 Chestnut Street
> Philadelphia, PA 19104

> **Phone:**
> (215) 895-2000

Pennsylvania State University

> **Degree:**
> Bachelor of Architecture

> **Location:**
> H. Campbell and Eleanor R. Stuckeman
> School of Architecture and Landscape Architecture
> The Pennsylvania State University
> 121 Stuckeman Family Building
> University Park, PA 16802

> **Phone:**
> (814) 865-9535

> **Email:**
> arch@psu.edu

Philadelphia University

    Degree:

    Bachelor of Architecture

    Location:

    School of Architecture - Philadelphia University

    School House Lane and Henry Ave

    Philadelphia, PA 19144

    Phone:

    (215) 951-2700

    Email:

    admissions@philau.edu

Temple University

    Degree:

    Bachelor of Architecture;

    Master of Architecture

    Location:

    Architecture Department

    Tyler School of Art - Temple University

    2001 North 13th Street

    Philadelphia, PA 19122

    Phone:

    (215) 777-9090

    Email:

    tylerart@temple.edu

University of Pennsylvania

Degree:

Master of Architecture

Location:

PennDesign - Architecture
102 Meyerson Hall
210 South 34th Street
Philadelphia, PA 19104

Phone:

(215) 898-5728

Email:

arch@design.upenn.edu

RHODE ISLAND:

Rhode Island School of Design

Degree:

Bachelor of Architecture;
Master of Architecture

Location:

Rhode Island School of Design
Two College Street
Providence, RI 02903

Phone:

(401) 454-6281

Email:

nroth@risd.edu

Roger Williams University
    Degree:
    Master of Architecture

    Location:
    RWU School of Architecture, Art and Historic Preservation
    One Old Ferry Road
    Bristol, RI 02809

    Phone:
    (401) 254-3605

    Email:
    saahp@rwu.edu

SOUTH CAROLINA:

Clemson University
    Degree:
    Master of Architecture

    Location:
    School of Architecture
    Clemson University
    3-130 Lee Hall
    Clemson, SC 29634

    Phone:
    (864) 656-1499

    Email:
    plauren@clemson.edu

TENNESSEE:

University of Memphis

Degree:

Candidate for Master of Architecture

Location:

Department of Architecture
404 Jones Hall
The University of Memphis
Memphis, TN 38152

Phone:

(901) 678-2724

Email:

architecture@memphis.edu

University of Tennessee at Knoxville

Degree:

Bachelor of Architecture;
Master of Architecture

Location:

College of Architecture and Design
Art & Architecture Building
1715 Volunteer Boulevard
Room 224
Knoxville, TN 37996

Phone:

(865) 974-5265

Email:

archinfo@utk.edu

TEXAS:

Prairie View A&M University

> **Degree:**
> Master of Architecture
>
> **Location:**
> Prairie View A&M University
> L.W. Minor Street, Room 100
> Prairie View, TX 77446
>
> **Phone:**
> (936) 261-9800

Rice University

> **Degree:**
> Bachelor of Architecture;
> Master of Architecture
>
> **Location:**
> Rice School of Architecture
> Rice University MS-50
> 6100 Main Street
> Houston, TX 7700
>
> **Phone:**
> (713) 348-4864
>
> **Email:**
> arch@rice.edu

Texas A&M University
Degree:
Master of Architecture

Location:
College of Architecture
3137 TAMU
College Station, TX 77843

Phone:
(979) 845-1015

Texas Tech University
Degree:
Master of Architecture

Location:
Texas Tech University College of Architecture
Mail Stop 42091
Lubbock, TX 7940

Phone:
(806) 742-3136

Email:
jess.schwintz@ttu.edu

University of Houston
>
> **Degree:**
>
> Bachelor of Architecture;
> Master of Architecture
>
> **Location:**
>
> Gerald D. Hines College of Architecture
> University of Houston
> 122 College of Architecture Bldg.
> Houston, TX 77204
>
> **Phone:**
> (713) 743-2400

University of Texas at Arlington
>
> **Degree:**
>
> Master of Architecture
>
> **Location:**
>
> University of Texas Arlington School of Architecture
> 601 W. Nedderman Dr., Suite 203
> Arlington, TX 76019
>
> **Phone:**
> (817) 272-2801
>
> **Email:**
> arch@uta.edu

University of Texas at Austin

Degree:

Bachelor of Architecture;
Master of Architecture

Location:

The University of Texas at Austin
School of Architecture
310 Inner Campus Drive Stop B7500
Austin, TX 78712

Phone:
(512) 471-1922

University of Texas at San Antonio

Degree:

Master of Architecture

Location:

The University of Texas at San Antonio
College of Architecture
501 W Cesar E. Chavez Blvd
San Antonio, TX 78207

Phone:
(210) 4580-3090

UTAH:

University of Utah
>   **Degree:**
>   Master of Architecture
>
>   **Location:**
>   The College of Architecture & Planning
>   375 S. 1530 E. Room 235
>   Salt Lake City, UT 84112
>
>   **Phone:**
>   (801) 581-8254
>
>   **Email:**
>   college@arch.utah.edu

VERMONT:

Norwich University
>   **Degree:**
>   Master of Architecture
>
>   **Location:**
>   Architecture & Art
>   158 Harmon Drive
>   Northfield, VT 05663
>
>   **Phone:**
>   (802) 485-2620
>
>   **Email:**
>   architectureart@norwich.edu

VIRGINIA:

Hampton University
> **Degree:**
> Master of Architecture
>
> **Location:**
> Hampton University
> Department of Architecture
> Hampton, VA 23668
>
> **Phone:**
> (757) 727-5440

University of Virginia
> **Degree:**
> Master of Architecture
>
> **Location:**
> School of Architecture
> Campbell Hall
> Rugby Road
> Charlottesville, VA 22903
>
> **Phone:**
> (434) 924-3715
>
> **Email:**
> arch-web@virginia.edu

Virginia Tech
> **Degree:**
> Bachelor of Architecture;
> Master of Architecture
>
> **Location:**
> School of Architecture & Design
> 201 Cowgill Hall (0205)
> Blacksburg, VA 24061
>
> **Phone:**
> (540) 231-5383
>
> **Email:**
> taylorw@vt.edu

WASHINGTON:

University of Washington
> **Degree:**
> Master of Architecture
>
> **Location:**
> University of Washington
> Department of Architecture
> 208 Gould Hall
> 3949 15th Ave NE
> Seattle, WA 98105
>
> **Phone:**
> (206) 543-3043
>
> **Email:**
> archdept@uw.edu

Washington State University

Degree:

Master of Architecture

Location:

School of Design & Construction
PO Box 642220
Washington State University
Pullman, WA 99164

Phone:
(509) 335-5539

Email:
soainfo@arch.wsu.edu

WISCONSIN:

University of Wisconsin at Milwaukee

Degree:

Master of Architecture

Location:

University of Wisconsin - Milwaukee
School Of Architecture and Urban Planning
2131 E. Hartford Avenue
Milwaukee , WI 53211

Phone:
(414) 229-4015

Email:
sarup-advising@uwm.edu

FINAL THOUGHTS

For most people, just attempting to get into a good university is very nerve-racking. So for you, attempting to get into the school you want, while trying to get into the architecture program you want, will be all that more daunting. I have read about people stressing to the point that they doubted themselves even being able to be accepted into any architecture school at all, only to come back and get into their first or second choice.

Be patient. Be confident. You will get there. When you are starting to doubt yourself, remember that you are being provided with everything you need to know here in order to be successful in your application and portfolio process. If you are one who has been able to get your hands on this book, you are not going in there blind like all of your other counterparts, so your portfolio will look that much better.

Let me leave you with this: NEVER GIVE UP ON YOUR DREAM TO BECOME AN ARCHITECT! It's never too early to start preparing, and it is never too late to get into architecture school.

ABOUT

Author

First off, I just want to tell a quick story, because to me, this story is the entire reason for this book's existence.

My wife and I had attended a couples dinner party with some friends of ours during the holidays a few years back. It wasn't a large party, probably about 10 or so couples in attendance. I remember that I was speaking with a woman and her husband—casually playing the small-talk game—when we came upon the subject of what I did for a living. I explained that I was in school, and I had recently been accepted into the architecture program. The lady then stated how great that must be and what an accomplishment it was. Come to find out later in our conversation, she had actually applied to architecture school some number of years back, but had been rejected.

Speaking with this woman made me think back on how I had applied to architecture school. After I had been accepted and was attending school, it seemed like it hadn't been that hard, but looking back—seriously analyzing my steps—I had realized that it took an insane amount of preparation, research, and planning to get that acceptance letter.

I don't doubt this woman could have made it into architecture school. She had the passion for it. She just lacked the help and the tools to get her there. I know now, that if she had read this book, she could very well have been an architect today.

As for myself, I'm just a guy who wants to share the insider tips that I've learned along the way. I host My School of Architecture (http://myschoolofarchitecture.com), where I have compiled a descriptive list of architecture schools, helpful posts, and a multitude of tools to help you along your way.

All of my hard work, perseverance, and research landed me into a professional architecture program with my first submission. To this day, I consider it one of my greatest accomplishments, because I worked so hard to make it happen. I want your acceptance letter to be one of your greatest accomplishments too!

Foreword Author

Marjorie K. Dickstein is a licensed architect with over 15 years of professional experience in her field. She received her Master of Architecture from Yale University, and holds additional degrees in Environmental Design and Urban Studies.

Licensed in two states, she is a LEED® AP BD+C, NCARB-Certified (facilitates architect license reciprocity in most states), Member of the AIA, and a Registered Interior Designer.

Her diverse portfolio of built work includes new university laboratory and computer science buildings; campus planning; public, private, and international schools; day cares and preschools; regional utility infrastructure; retail and customer service facilities; hospitality, resorts, restaurants; cultural and community centers; elderly housing, assisted living, healthcare; offices, corporate headquarters; and new homes, residential additions, and renovations.

...And a corn maze!

SHOW YOUR SUPPORT

If you enjoyed this book, or found it helpful, please write a quick review to let us know what you thought.

For those purchasing this on Kindle, you will see a review page following shortly after this (please take a second and let us know what you think).

For others who purchased a hardcopy or other electronic format, you can write your reviews at http://www.amazon.com/dp/B009FEVACE.

Good luck in your journey to architecture school! I wish you the best!

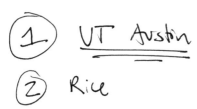

① <u>UT Austin</u>

② Rice

③ UF

4. Texas A&M

5. USF

6. New Mexico, Montana, Wash U →

↘ ↘ out-of-state
   and dependent
       on scholarships

Made in the USA
Lexington, KY
11 February 2015